I, WHO HAVE LEFT YOU

I, WHO HAVE LEFT YOU

A Lover's Memoir

Susan Freeman

iUniverse, Inc.
Bloomington

I, Who Have Left You
A Lover's Memoir

iUniverse books may be ordered through booksellers or by contacting:

iUniverse
1663 Liberty Drive
Bloomington, IN 47403
www.iuniverse.com
1-800-Authors (1-800-288-4677)

ISBN: 978-1-4697-9182-1 (sc)
ISBN: 978-1-4697-9184-5 (e)
ISBN: 978-1-4697-9183-8 (dj)

Library of Congress Control Number: 2012904506

Printed in the United States of America

iUniverse rev. date: 3/22/2012

For Leslie

I, who have left you, always take great care in the measure of your devotion. I, who have watched you grow and have watched you enchant my essence, take great pride in your accomplishments. Do not be afraid to spread your wings in earth years. You are but apart from me in time, apart from each other. There will be no fault finding. You will subscribe to truth, to energy, to healing, and to love, for truly love conquers all.

You were not afraid when I needed you to be brave. You did not show fear, even in your younger days. I have myself left. I am connected to you. When you speak, I hear you. When you think, I think with you, and when your heart is heavy, I feel you. I feel your grace and your love and your tenderness.

You do not need to seek me out, dear one. I am here, and you are the love. You have my blessing to live, to life.

—Leslie

Contents

Prologue   xi

Up on the Farm   1

A Courtship of Letters   31

Arabia   65

Letters from the Land of Enchantment   91

Stage IV   109

The Passing of a Star   133

Soul Encounters   147

Acknowledgments   179

Prologue

Every story has two parts: the telling and the hearing. I want to tell you my story and have you hear what I have learned from loving a man named Leslie Freeman. Our story is told through our letters. I can visualize myself typing my first letter to Leslie in 1975, sitting in a farmhouse kitchen in North Dakota, and reading my last letter from him, on the day he left this earth, twenty-seven years later.

We were two people who met and recognized the potential for a great love, but we were both married. It took nine years for me to realize that our love was worth the risk and toll of divorce. We married in 1984 and spent our first eighteen wedded months working in a hospital in the mountainous region of Saudi Arabia. When we returned to the United States, New Mexico, the Land of Enchantment, became our home. Eighteen years after we wed, Leslie committed an act of self-deliverance to escape the final ravages of lung cancer. His last letters to family and friends chronicled the odyssey preceding what he termed "the final, greatest experience of life."

After he passed away, I wanted to join him. Instead, I worked with a grief counselor. At the end of our sessions, she told me about a clairaudient, one who channels messages from the other side. The first message I received from the soul of Leslie began, "*I, who have left you.*"

Our story hasn't ended, as I have continued to receive his messages in the nine years since he crossed over to the outer realm, as he refers to the other side. The messages guide me, encourage me to go on, and sometimes make me smile. When he passed away, I did not believe in life after death. I now do.

I have chosen to tell our story by writing to Leslie's oldest granddaughter, Sylvie. These letters do not exist outside of this memoir but serve as a vehicle for context, explaining my feelings in describing Leslie and the love we share. The letters and journals identified as written by Leslie and Susan do exist, as do the taped messages from the other side. Leslie had two daughters, Martha and Amy. Martha has three children, Leslie's grandchildren—Sylvie, Rosa, and Ethan. The names of other individuals have been changed.

Leslie encourages me to tell you our story, for, as he relates, "*if truth be told, it is stranger than fiction and more beautiful than any story can be.*"

Up on the Farm

Susan Freeman to Sylvie Frank, July 2010

My dear Sylvie,

Congratulations! A graduate of Wellesley, no less. You join a prestigious group of women who have "made a difference in the world," to quote the website. I number you among them already, Sylvie. I think back to the last time I saw your dad, and he told me how amazing he thought you were, such an admirable person. He didn't say "beautiful"; he didn't have to, for that is *prima facie*. Know I will always care for you. I love you because of who you are, who you will become, and because you are the grandchild of my beloved Leslie and daughter of his beloved Martha.

Not too often, for it is emotional, I look back at Freeman family photos. There is one of your Grandpa Leslie holding you for the first time. How proud he would be of you, Sylvie.

He was quite taken with turquoise and would have approved of my choice of a gift to commemorate your graduation. When I part from this worldly plane, I will leave you the gold bracelet your grandfather gave me as a wedding gift.

Armed with a degree, world travels, broken hearts (others hopefully, not yours), internal and external beauty, many who love and admire you, may the life you create be a successful one. Enjoy life as you live it. A simple platitude, true, but it does take concerted effort to live in the present moment.

May your joys, your accomplishments, and the loves you have had and will have far outnumber the sorrows and grief you will undoubtedly experience.

Susan

Sylvie to Susan, September 15, 2010

Dear Susan,

Thank you for the lovely necklace, the kind words, and the thoughts of my grandfather. I can't believe how long it has been since I last saw you and how much has happened since. I have been living in New York City for the past month, working as an editorial assistant for a publishing house. I love my job, my life in the city, and being in a position to make new friends. Tonight, I am hosting my first dinner party.

If you have time, please tell me more about Grandpa Leslie and your life together. I think of you both often.

Love, Sylvie

Susan to Sylvie, October 10, 2010

Dear Sylvie,

You know me as an older, proper lady, given to fits of everything in its place, and in a certain order—in short, anal-retentive. Would it surprise you that when I was thirty-six, I was told by the American consul general to Saudi Arabia that I reminded him of a nun who didn't wear underwear? Or that somewhere in the mountains of California, my name is inscribed in a book of motorcycle riders who reached the summit of a steep mountain pass?

You probably don't know that I was married to a man named Stewart Gillon before I married your grandfather or that your grandfather and I wrote letters to one another over a twenty-seven-year span. Before I share our letters with you, I'll tell you about my life before Leslie.

I think that most of us want to believe in magical tales of love and romance, even as cynical and realistic as we have become. We want to believe that the girl will find the boy of her dreams and live happily ever after. My dream man was tall, slender, and smart, and he loved me as I loved him. I knew that someday he would find me. Maybe girls like me were prone to be dreamers.

There was just one boyfriend during my high school years. This was during the sixties in Southern California. Popular girls were slim with straight blonde hair. Mine was short and wavy brown, subject to frizz on a foggy morn. The music of my youth was the Beach Boys and the Beatles, but I preferred classical. I sang in the church choir, and the director ushered me to the back row with the instructions "don't try so hard."

By the time my teens ended, my unknown dream man had not found me. Instead, there was Stewart Gillon, whom I met on New Year's Eve 1967. I was nineteen; he was twenty-seven. He was a practical joker, and I learned how to have a good time. He taught me to handle and shoot firearms, ride dirt bikes in the California desert, and drink beer. Years later, someone asked me why I married him; it was because he made me laugh.

Two days before our wedding, groundskeepers aerated and spread manure around the church lawn, a portentous sign of our life together.

Ever-agreeable at the time, I feigned excitement for our honeymoon, which was spent deer hunting in Utah. Our bridal suite was a blue tent equipped with Coleman's finest and decorated with an inflatable Heinz ketchup bottle, a bit of color amid the snow. I never told Stewart that I saw several deer pass within yards of our tent without raising my .243 Remington bolt-action rifle. Our marriage might have ended then.

When I married Stewart, I was committed to him emotionally and mentally, but I didn't feel any physical passion. I didn't know what passion was. A few months before our wedding, I had the sinking feeling that I was making a mistake. In the back of my mind, I realized that I had given up finding my dream man. After we married, I quit college and went to work.

The first four years of our marriage were fun. Stewart worked for a food manufacturer, and I worked for two ministers, riding to work on my bicycle, miniskirt over my jeans. Several times, we made treks to Stewart's parents' farm in northeastern North Dakota. I liked the prairie and the half hours Stewart's dad, Pappy, let me spend driving his tractor to cultivate the summer fallow. When Pappy had a heart attack early in 1973, Stewart and I went back to put in the crop. The fun half hours were now long days, and the appeal waned. We had just moved to the South Bay area of Southern California and purchased a small condo. Upon our return from helping Pappy, I looked for a new job.

On June 14, 1973, your grandfather interviewed me for a job. After all these years, I remember what he wore, how I thought that, even if I never saw him again, I would never forget him. He was the dream man I hadn't waited for, sitting right there in front of me.

These were years before my name had the BS after it. I worked as a clerk in one of the ten offices of a regional medical facility. Leslie (Mr. Freeman to me) was the regional administrator and visited our office twice a month. I eagerly anticipated these late-afternoon visits and always stood by the window to watch him as he walked to his car. In time, I became a troubleshooter for the facilities, training new office staff and writing office procedure manuals. Occasionally, I accompanied Mr. Freeman on day trips to one or more of the facilities.

One August day in 1974, I joined him on a trip to Santa Barbara, and it was then that I knew I loved him. The first time he assisted me out of his car, lightly touching my back, the sparks flew. I had no idea then if I was the only one who felt it or whether he was conscious of it also. Truly, it was a novel feeling for me. I thought, after my sexual experiences, that sparks were a fantasy relegated to trashy novels. How wrong I was.

When Pappy announced his pending retirement in January 1975, Stewart decided to return to his boyhood home and farm—with or without me. I did not want to leave my family, my friends, my job, and most of all, Mr. Freeman. I planned on giving a month's notice, as we were to depart in April. In February I went with Mr. Freeman on a day trip to Bakersfield, and on our return trip home, he offered me a job as the regional training manager. I was both thrilled and deflated; all I could say was, "I cannot, for I am leaving you." It sounds made up, even after all these years, but those were my very words, not the job, but *you.*

His response left me speechless: "Do you know that I have wanted to be your lover?"

We stopped in the little town of Gorman for a drink and to talk. I felt numb with excitement and dread at the thought of leaving him. We held hands for the first time.

Over the space of a month, we seriously discussed having a day and a night together, a gift with no strings attached. Would it hurt the other people in our lives? Would it hurt us?

I confess that we were unfaithful to the people we had married, one of whom was your grandmother. I don't ask to be forgiven because I never regretted it, not once. It was the passion and tenderness I had never known. We were wrong about the no strings attached, though. I never got over it. I thought I could. I so wanted Leslie to ask me to stay, to say, "Don't go to North Dakota." He didn't; instead he told me to be a winner.

The "what ifs" of one's life—what if I hadn't been so conflicted and torn between the two men I loved? What if I had stayed and not gone to North Dakota? Leslie told me, years later, that I had to go to North Dakota. He just didn't think it would take me as long as it did to be a winner.

Stewart and I arrived at the Gillon farm in April of 1975. When I got out of the U-Haul truck, it began to snow. Another omen I did not heed.

Almost nine years passed before your grandfather and I married. Though I don't ask forgiveness, Sylvie, please know that I never wanted to hurt anyone.

Susan

Sylvie to Susan, November 1, 2010

Dear Susan,

After reading your letter, I realize how little I know about Grandpa—and even less about you. I have only known you as Grandpa's wife, and you two were married before I was born. I never thought to ask if you were married before or how you and Grandpa met.

My first memories of you and Grandpa are when you visited us after we moved east. I must have been eight or nine. I remember that he let me help him barbecue and showed me how to decorate the serving platter with parsley. Maybe that's how my love of cooking began!

I am an editorial assistant for a publishing house of books for young people. I read many types of manuscripts but no love letters.

Please keep writing and sharing more about your lives.

Sylvie

Susan to Sylvie, November 20, 2010

Dear Sylvie,

I thought about copying the letters in my box of treasures and sending them to you. The originals will become yours after I leave this earth. It is a comfort to me, even now, to see his handwriting, to hold what he once created. A few years before his death, he began using the computer to write and save his letters.

Since Leslie passed away, I have been transcribing our letters and saving them electronically, with the thought of writing about us, sharing our story, for it is a story not only about love but about what happens to us when we pass away.

After my mom died, I found a journal she had written, describing her life growing up on a farm in Virginia; her first marriage to my brother's father, who was killed in World War II; and her life with my dad. I was stunned when I read that she had married my father two weeks after they met. Knowing them as I thought I did, I can't imagine them ever being impetuous. I don't even know where they were married. Their siblings and cousins have all passed away. The whys and questions I have will never be answered. Thus, I will begin sending you our letters, and if you have questions, you can ask this living person.

Leslie described himself as a square in a world with few corners left. He was the proverbial marcher who didn't need a drum, didn't notice or care if his steps didn't align with others'. I would describe him as erudite, good-looking, courtly, an untrained artist, and an elegant tennis player. He sounds perfect, but he had his faults. Sometimes his serendipitous nature took precedence over his earning power. My financial laments were met with "we have everything but money." And, as you know, he smoked. He started smoking cigars as a college freshman listening to live radio broadcasts of the Metropolitan Opera. Eventually, he switched to a pipe. He told me there were only two things in his life he couldn't control: smoking and me.

Attached is my first letter to your grandfather, written thirty-five years ago. Behind the expressed words were the unwritten ones, the ones of love and longing. They were sent to his office, typed on a prized IBM Selectric. I kept a dictionary by my side, ever-mindful of the wordsmith I was trying to impress.

Susan

Susan to Leslie Freeman, June 3, 1975

Dear Leslie,

Pappy, my father-in-law, tells me, "Some folks say there ain't no hell, but they never farmed, so they cain't tell." I agree.

The Gillon farm occupies five quarters, eight hundred acres—a small farm in northeastern North Dakota. Stewart said it was once known as the pink farm. When he was a kid, he and Pappy occasionally pulled vehicles out of the ditch as passersby, marveling at the Pepto-Bismol colors of the house, failed to keep their eyes on the road. Inside is also pink. After we've applied gallons of white paint, only the pink toilet, tub, and sink remain. Less than a thousand square feet, the house is two-storied with a gable roof. The musty, mint-green basement contains a shower, storm cellar, and diesel storage tank. A city visitor commented that the shower reminded her of the one in *Psycho*. Fortunately, I never saw the movie, nor do I fear the spiders who continually rebuild their woven homes in the confines of the shower's cement block and Formica paneling. My favorite room is the small living room, which has two large picture windows facing south and east where I watch the world light up each morning.

Farmland in this part of North Dakota is flat. We joke that we can see the lights of a town twenty miles away. I think an apt description of my feelings thus far is this: "I have never been able to see so far and see so little."

The farming community residents are kind to me. As a Southern California transplant, I am not accustomed to everyone knowing me or about me. Sometimes, I think they know what happens to me before I do! I chafe at being Mrs. Stewart Gillon. I just want to be Susan. My attire consists of T-shirts, jeans, and boots, with my hair tucked into a railroad engineer's cap. The only feminine adornments are my pearl earrings. I wear them whether I am changing oil in the tractor, greasing zerks, or shoveling grain.

My first field assignment was to ready the "east eighty" for planting. Only pit stops were allowed; we worked until dark. I came back to the farmyard in the early afternoon to refuel. Sitting up straight, I shifted to low gear and readied my boot on the brake, inching the tractor down to the gashouse. The cultivator extends twelve feet on each side of the tractor. I was careful not to get too close, yet I got close enough for the hose to reach the tractor's tank. The routine is as follows: Climb up the gashouse ladder, get the hose, turn on the valve, climb down, and begin fueling. Do not overfill. Now, repeat the process in reverse. The worst part comes last. If I don't back away from the gashouse straight, the cultivator jackknifes.

This particular afternoon, my back up was straight; I felt relief, until I heard a crunching rip of metal. The lugs on the tractor tire caught the gashouse door handle. The door no longer rested in its frame. Panic. I did not want to incur Stewart's ire. Removing the mangled hinge, I ran the hundred yards to the Quonset. It was my first experience with a vise grip and sledgehammer. Twenty minutes later, the hinges were back on and the door rehung. Observant eyes might notice several areas of missing pink paint. Stewart's never did.

Though this mishap was not observed, my many others were. Attempting to seed too close to a slough, Stewart mired the tractor in mud. I was summoned to pull him out. He hooked a chain to his muddied tractor and one to mine. He gave explicit instructions on which gear to use, how fast to go, how far to pull—and I executed exactly as instructed. He did not tell me to first take the slack out of the chain. Oh, can he yell when he's mad.

I do try, but I am an incompetent farmhand.

Susan

Sylvie to Susan, December 1, 2010

Dear Susan,

Hope you had a nice Thanksgiving. We did. I went home for the long weekend, and we all pitched in to make our favorite dishes.

I remember seeing a picture of you with long hair, the one when you and Grandpa married. But I can't picture you on a farm or driving a tractor. It doesn't fit my image of you.

Sylvie

Susan to Sylvie, December 7, 2010

Dear Sylvie,

Your grandfather's favorite meal was roast turkey with all the Cash (my maiden name) family's favorite side dishes. The Christmas before he passed away, he taught our friend Diane and me how to perfectly carve the turkey breast. The first year without him, we followed his instructions, crying as we carved.

As humorously as I attempt to describe my experiences in North Dakota, the nine years I spent on the farm were the unhappiest ones of my life. Only when I mowed the grass did my nerves cease their overtime transmissions. Even a slight whiff of freshly mowed grass still transports me back to the farm. The job consumed hours each week, spent riding the International Harvester cub cadet. I would relax, let my senses revel in the unaccustomed sounds of birds and visions of unobstructed sky and green: green grass, green trees, green hedges, green grain stalks, and green leafy vegetables. Three times in my life have I experienced utter happiness, a happiness approaching ecstasy. One was mowing the grass, alone, on the farm. It was the closest I ever felt to God.

I never forgot Leslie's comment to me before I left for North Dakota: "be a winner." I tried not to let on how unhappy I was.

Susan

Susan to Leslie, June 18, 1975

Dear Leslie,

Farming in this area is totally weather-dependent. It is the focal point of conversation, the common thread binding us together.

We received our first measurable precipitation last Friday night. Stewart and I sat in the kitchen without power and watched a turbulent sky, flashing with lightning and racked by thunder. The rain hit like a wave. Within fifteen minutes, we received an inch and two tenths. Sitting in the dark watching the rain, we felt little splatters: the picture window is not watertight. Since we were a bit agitated, we were glad of something constructive to do. As we arranged towels and buckets, we heard what farmers fear most: the clatter of hail. Fortunately, the stones were small and lasted only minutes. What a night! Those churning clouds gave birth to a tornado, which touched down fifteen miles south of the county seat and demolished a farm. In all, we received two and a half inches of welcome rain. Our verdant world is safe for the time being.

Blessings can be expensive: the crops need weed spray. We had hired a ground sprayer, but with the moisture, an aerial sprayer is required—at an additional sixty cents an acre. Projected weed expense is now negated. One must be resilient in this occupation. The aerial sprayer has a unique collection policy. If a farmer fails to pay, he sends a statement stamped with "pay up, you cheap bastard."

Caught a portion of *The Johnny Carson Show* on the one station we receive with him posing as a nude bowler behind an appropriately placed bowling ball. He was asked, "What's the biggest problem you have in a nudist colony?" His retort: "Finding a place to tuck your napkin."

May your days be rewarding,

Susan

Sylvie to Susan, December 11, 2010

Dear Susan,

We didn't have a television in our home until I was in high school. Mom and Dad purchased an old TV and VHS player so we could watch movies. I felt deprived then but not now, and it surprises me how much time people spend watching TV.

Sylvie

Susan to Sylvie, December 15, 2010

Dear Sylvie,

I've never been much of a TV watcher either, even now. Growing up, I was allowed to watch *Lassie*, my favorite *Roy Rogers*, and we all watched *Bonanza*.

Those first years on the farm, I remember being so tired, wondering how they did it all years ago. When I returned from my tractor assignments, there were clothes to wash, food to prepare, and finally a shower and bed. In time, my body became acclimated to the roar and jostle of the tractor, but it usually took an hour for my ears to quit humming. I attribute my diminished hearing to those hours spent driving the tractor. Then and now, my nightly enjoyments and relaxation are music and reading. My subversive friend, music, resides with me wherever I live.

Attached are letters Leslie and I exchanged through the summer and fall. The first describes an event that proved financially devastating, one from which Stewart and I never recovered. I didn't know it at the time, of course.

Susan

Susan to Leslie, July 14, 1975

Dear Leslie,

A month ago, we ordered twenty gallons of exterior paint to cover the pink. Last week, we began with a new paint sprayer, a regulator, and a good frame of mind to face this dreaded ordeal. We opened up the first gallon and, even with vigorous stirring, Vermont Red looked orange. Stewart didn't think it was too bad, but when he asked my opinion, without hesitation, I told him it was hideous. Gone the good frame of mind, as I most always agree with him. He told me to paint an old board, and we took it to our neighbor's farm—whose color we had tried to duplicate.

Placing the board next to his Quonset, Lloyd commented, "Gee, but that's orange."

Bless him. I was mute, envisioning the pink farm becoming known as the orange farm. The paint supplier would not take the twenty gallons back, as it was a special order. They did tell us that, if some other poor soul placed an order for this color (hope they are color-blind), they would utilize our ample supply. We purchased another twenty gallons of a color we both liked—from a different supplier—and, in one day, we sprayed five buildings. Only two buildings remain unpainted, due to intermittent rain showers the past week.

We have had sufficient moisture the past six weeks, and the crops look as if they will exceed our speculated yield of thirty bushels to the acre. During these six weeks, we have had some unnerving storms, brief but impressive, realizing what havoc they could create. One such storm hit the farm last Saturday with eighty-mile-per-hour winds blowing every which direction. In fifteen minutes, we received almost a half inch, and a few hail stones that were too small to do any damage. Stewart and I stood in the garage and watched. When the sun emerged, a double rainbow melded sky to earth, and we went back to our books. An hour later, we received a phone call from a farmer looking for Pappy, who writes insurance. He wanted to report hail damage on his farmhouse and buildings. Stewart asked him where he lived. It was a mile south of the quarter of land we are buying from Stewart's aunt. After all the other storms, we had driven to our land but not this time.

We immediately drove the five miles south; I kept thinking, *No, please no.* The crop was completely destroyed. What had been 111 acres of three-foot durum and barley was now stubble, sliced to four- and six-inch ribbons by hail the size of golf balls. Farming is still a cyclically risky business.

The storm was five miles wide and forty miles in length, destroying some 750 quarters of cropland. Most did not have hail insurance, as this area is low risk. We were included in the most, as our quarter had not been hailed upon since 1917. Hail insurance is costly—with and without.

Enjoy your vacation, and may you continue to impress them with your outdoor culinary skills.

Susan

Leslie to Susan, July 20, 1975

Dear Susan,

How frustrating to persist in the belief that hard work, a good life, and clean living will be rewarded. Rude experience tries to teach us fact from myth time and again, but still we persist. What parent has not labored the myth as fact to his child in order to solicit ethical behavior? The Roman Church tried to conceal reality by promising the faithful just reward, but not in this life. The whole Western concept of justice—that the individual is responsible for the consequences of his own acts—is threatened if we don't believe. We want to believe. The loss of faith can be painful and tends to cynicism and bitterness and eventually to fatalism.

Faith is important to the young and essential to the aged. How else can you expect to find the courage to start again, even with the odds against you? How can the old accept the indignities of aging without the strength of belief? No, Susan, there is no Santa Claus. But can you accept at this time in your life that it is important you continue to believe in Santa Claus?

Leslie

Susan to Leslie, July 27, 1975

Dear Leslie,

At 8:00 p.m., a gentle rain, soft music, alone. Five-gallon bags of green beans finally stacked in the freezer, the hours spent in preparing them also contemplating your letter.

Our town, population 102, not including the farming community, is nine miles northeast of the Gillon farm. It consists of a small grocery store, an International Harvester implement company, a post office, two grain elevators, and two thriving bars. I can attest to the town's reputation—you are six drinks behind before you get out of your truck. Tommy's Bar is the favorite; until the thirties, it was a bank, but after the banker was strung up, the empty vault was and is stocked with gold of a liquid variety, a fitting tribute to barley growers.

Peas to be picked, trepidation of black clouds with harvest beginning only weeks away.

Yes, Leslie, I do believe in Santa Claus.

Susan

Leslie to Susan, August 20, 1975

Dear Susan,

For the better part of a decade, six of us, with me being the only nonphysician, rented horses and pack animals and ascended the Sierra Mountains east of Bishop for an extended weekend. We each had assignments, mine being cook. Individually, we did our own thing during the day, meeting back at camp for a preprandial cocktail hour.

On our ascent, one of the horses sustained a deep slash on its foreleg. With a pathologist, an anesthesiologist, a pediatrician, a gynecologist, and a surgeon (I steadied the head), the horse's wound was efficiently sterilized, stitched, and bandaged. We felt quite smug until we realized that the emergency medical kit was depleted. Fortunately, no other mishaps ensued.

Upon my return, I flew to Las Vegas to negotiate for a prospective dialysis center in the hospital. Rather than successfully completing the negotiation, I was hospitalized for probable pneumonitis. Lab results were inconclusive, except for an iron deficiency with Geritol prescribed. Losing battle with Nurse Ratched over my pipe, I resorted to drawing, a childhood activity long since put aside.

Back at work, pipe in hand.

Leslie

Susan to Leslie, August 26, 1975

Dear Leslie,

In the spring, farmers pray for no rain until seeding is finished. During June and July, ample rain is prayed for; a few weeks in August—prayers for *no* rain and hot weather to herald the advent of harvest. After eight straight days of sixteen hours driving the combine, I unabashedly prayed for rain (just a few sprinkles). It rained for half an hour this afternoon. Only ninety acres left to combine. Plowing is next, a slow job, three acres an hour, and then a week of surreptitious ditching, as county officials have nixed the creation of new ditches.

Tuesday night, I had an hour break and, before returning to the field, picked up the mail, a welcomed letter. Geritol, ugh, visions of the smiling TV countenances that owe it to themselves and their families. I wonder if they ever smelled the stuff. Remembering that, in your youth, you drank tomato juice with chopped liver, I am sure you can tolerate Geritol.

Our gardening efforts have been successful. Not utilizing the yield of one's garden, however, can create deep-seated anxiety over being wasteful (costs only a few dollars for a large canning kettle and jars). Better yet, one starts counting friends, casual acquaintances, on whom to bestow the fruits of one's harvest. The only vegetable we let get out of hand, literally, is the zucchini. I don't even like zucchini. They are now two to three feet long and some six inches in diameter! Stewart solved this problem. He sent a huge potato sack full of these overgrown wonders to his aunt. When they arrived, she was entertaining her church circle, and the ladies each wanted one of the biggest zucchini they had ever seen! Expiated after all.

Our tomato plants number twelve, and each plant has between fifteen and twenty fruits. My enjoyment of watching them mature diminished when I heard rustling retreats: snakes. I used to be able to tolerate them with respect. Ever the prankster, Stewart dropped one in the combine with me. It immediately slithered out of sight. After three hours of driving with my feet firmly planted on the windows, my tolerance turned to dire anxiety.

Please keep drinking Geritol.

Susan

Leslie to Susan, September 10, 1975

Dear Susan,

Your gardening efforts remind me of the amount of money spent on landscaping the yard last year at our newly occupied home. The vegetable garden was enthusiastically enjoined, in hopes of satisfying some macho conceit that all things are possible to those who try hard enough. The beds were laid out in such fashion that each was readily accessible without having to stomp through them to weed, nourish, or harvest by hand. The end result was a series of raised beds in such geometric rigidity that it resembled nothing so much as a cemetery with a row of freshly dug graves. We did enjoy some fresh leaf lettuce, radishes, and, of course, zucchini; otherwise, the harvest was meager.

I was reminded of my mother's agricultural heritage and thought back to the early 1940s, when patriotic urban dwellers were urged by the federal government to plow up their horticultural yards and plant "victory gardens" to help the war effort. At Mother's direction, we dug a garden under the clothesline in the backyard of our rented house in Flushing, New York, and planted a variety of vegetables, which we children were encouraged to tend. In the fall, when the potato crop was dug up, we found some as big as golf balls, some as big as marbles, and in addition, as Mother related to her mother, quite a few little ones.

We children were spared the embarrassment of further efforts in this direction, as well as any possible future career as farmers, by the cessation of hostilities.

You have my admiration for your gardening prowess.

Leslie

P.S. What is a zerk?

Susan to Leslie, September 21, 1975

Dear Leslie,

At 4:00 p.m., we finished plowing the last field. We started on September 4 and have not taken a day off. There is an unspoken law in this country: one does not work on Sundays. We do not adhere to the law, but at times I think we should, for as the days wear on, the tiredness increases, tempers shorten, and minor problems seem major. It has not been a happy week, but today has been a good one, accomplishment for another cycle completed.

Stewart left for town to celebrate plowing's end, and I picked up the mail. My celebration is your letter. "What is a zerk?"

There are eleven zerks on the tractor, thirteen on the cultivator, ten on the plow, forty on the combine. *Zerk* is not listed in *Webster's New World College Dictionary*. I questioned Stewart regarding the spelling, *zerk*. He first heard it from his father, so I jokingly said, "Maybe he meant *you jerk*," which he did not appreciate.

A zerk is a grease fitting, a small protuberance to which a grease gun is affixed to convey grease to a joint. How's that?

Forewarned of last night's frost, my affection for the tomato plants and array of flowers was put to the test. I covered them all, but even with burlap sacks, 26 degrees took its toll, the only tarnish to this day.

Tomorrow, the first day of fall. Thousands of geese feed in nearby fields, and in a few weeks the first snow will fly, our signal to return to Southern California.

Susan

Susan to Sylvie, December 18, 2010

Dear Sylvie,

Reading my letters to Leslie, the ones I have attached and the ones I put aside, it appears that I never had any fun or did anything other than work. Not so. Lloyd, the farmer whose colors we attempted to duplicate, holds his own special chamber in my heart. I remember the first time I met Lloyd. I didn't like him because he made fun of me. Shy, sensitive Susan. Didn't take long though for him to make me laugh. Over the years, I have internally thanked him for teaching me to laugh at myself. Truly, one can survive most anything if one's sense of humor remains intact. After abdominal surgery, I was lying in a hospital bed, in a lot of pain, and I started crying. The tears were pooling in my ears, and I remembered a song I heard, imprisoned in the tractor. It went like this: "I have tears in my ears from lying flat on my back crying over you." I laughed and once again silently thanked Lloyd for his priceless gift. The nurse soon came, and oh, morphine is a wonderful drug.

One more Lloyd story. During my last career as a traveling auditor, we used to swap stories to fill the many hours spent waiting in airports and driving to wary audit sites. I had lots of Lloyd stories to relate. One midsummer night, I stayed too late at Lloyd's farm talking (and drinking wine) with Lloyd and his mother. Lloyd went to bed, his mother and I talked longer, and I eventually dozed off on the couch. Around two or so when I awakened, I took off for the Gillon farm. Well, with the dark and the noises, I started running on the dirt road, and with my somewhat unsteady gait, my shoe was flung into the ditch. Too concerned with the dark and unknown noises to find it, I continued home, no one the wiser. Should have known, Lloyd arrived the next morning with my thong. Nothing escaped him.

As I was explaining this to a young auditor, her face took on a shocked look. I asked her what was wrong. She said, "How did you lose your thong in the ditch?"

When I think of thongs, I think of shoes—not underwear. I now use the term flip-flops. I digress, but I wanted you to know I do have some funny memories of my years on the farm.

I have been tempted to fast-forward to the time when Leslie and I married, but how do I explain the nine years from when we professed our love for one another until we married? We only exchanged letters my first two years on the farm. Stewart and I returned to Southern California the first two winters, working to support ourselves and to bring back a little savings each spring.

Within a month of my return to Southern California in 1976, Leslie and his employer parted company. Our season of working together had ended. We met infrequently, and, for the first time, Leslie spoke of his unhappiness, of his decision to seek a divorce. He assured me that the divorce was not because of us, not because of his love for me. It was because of money and the expectations placed upon him to keep obtaining better and bigger jobs, homes, and status. Your grandmother would someday inherit a sizable estate, and he feared that she would attempt to control him, even subconsciously, with money. It was not the life he wanted.

He was offered a job as finance director of a hospital in New Mexico. In February 1977, Leslie moved to Albuquerque, alone, and filed for divorce. He was forty-seven. The Land of Enchantment, as hokey as it sounds, would become his most beloved place. He asked me to join him.

Attached is my reply.

Susan

Susan to Leslie, March 19, 1977

Dear Leslie,

The torture of the mind is in sorting everything out and, if possible, setting aside all the conflicting emotions to determine who one is and what one wants. I realize I am alone; there is no one else I can rely on to take care of me, and nothing stays the same. External security doesn't exist; only what you create inside—and that, too, changes. I sometimes wonder what is wrong in me that so often I don't enjoy or can't relax enough to accept my own existence. I create dream worlds, especially the last two years. I lived on the farm dreaming of the day when I would return to you, yet all the while clinging to the security of Stewart, despite the fights—and he had only my shell.

In doing this, I have hurt all of us. You are the stronger person, Leslie, sure of yourself and knowing what you want for the rest of your life.

You were right to state that I was on the downhill path, with the barriers and falls I created, and through you, I saw a way out. Yes, the guilt has been tremendous, as it has been for you. I can't do it for you, through you—only through me. I am racked with indecision, Leslie. You told me I could only come to you if I had made a clean cut; I cannot. You are thinking I am acting out of fear, loss of security. Yes, in part I am. And you would not want me like this. What bothers me most is the hurt I caused, and because of what I am doing, I lose you.

My loving you is no dream, Leslie. You are a part of me. You have been my source of strength, and perhaps unknowingly, I have relied so much on you. I am going to live each day, no fairy tales in the future, only trying to be honest. I will go back to the farm and try to create a life for myself. If I see trying with my mind not just my body still fails, then perhaps I won't feel the guilt. And I can't shake the guilt, for it is true that my mind was never there.

Leslie, forgive me. I know I won't be able to live forgetting you, for my concern and care and love for you live in me. You have told me you didn't believe there was just one person for any of us. We have shared much, our physical and mental communion.

Your decision is made, my darling Leslie, may your life be richer. Part of my love for you is a deep respect and admiration. Nothing equals the despair of the last few months. You said it would make us stronger people. We both must learn to live with our choice and whatever rewards and mistakes this choice will bring. I know you well enough to realize that you did this for yourself but also with hope for us.

It is beyond me to find a suitable closing other than the happiest, most pleasurable moments of my life you have given to me.

Susan

Susan to Sylvie, December 22, 2010

Dear Sylvie,

Over the course of the next seven years, I did take those happy, pleasurable memories, and I relived them in tractors, combines, and during continuing sad times on the farm, silently chanting what had become my mantra: be a winner. The memories helped me endure. So much for living in the present, as I have told you to do.

In an attempt to salvage our marriage, Stewart agreed that I could finish college, as long as I paid my own way. With a student loan supporting me, I returned to college in 1978 and graduated from the University of North Dakota in 1980 with a degree in accounting; it was a confidence booster to graduate *magna cum laude*. Five letters soon trailed after my name, BS, CPA.

Leslie and I met again in the fall of 1980. It was a surprise meeting, arranged by a mutual friend. Leslie had flown to Los

Angeles for a job interview, and I was spending the winter doing part-time work in Southern California. Our friend invited us for dinner, and afterward, I drove Leslie back to his motel room. Your grandfather placed me in a chair in the middle of the room and told me that there would be no further communication between us unless I divorced Stewart.

"When we two parted in silence and tears..."

In 1982, instead of returning to California during the winter to supplement our income, I stayed in North Dakota, moved to the county seat during the winter months, and worked for Production Credit Association (PCA) preparing taxes for farmers.

The summer of 1983, Stewart and I went on a bus trip to St. Paul with my coworkers for a company meeting. We had one of our increasingly frequent fights. After the initial outburst, there was silence. We could go for days without speaking to one another.

On the return trip, imbued with a few too many, Stewart told my coworkers, "Susan is so cold, when she walks by the furnace, it kicks in."

Funny in retrospect; it wasn't then. I sought solace in the two-by-three bus bathroom and cried. Divorce now became a frequently visited subject in my mind.

In August 1983, I called Leslie in Albuquerque, but still I was the coward. This time, your grandfather moved on. In November, he accepted a job as the accounting manager of a hospital located in the mountainous southwestern region of Saudi Arabia. Before he departed, he returned my letters.

New Year's Eve 1967, Stewart and I met. New Year's Eve 1983, I decided to petition for divorce. It was the day the slow learner finally mastered the lesson. My faltering steps ceased. It was also the day the attached letter from Leslie arrived.

May you enjoy your holiday season, Sylvie. I am sending a small token to your folks' home for Christmas, as your grandfather liked to say, an esteem of my token. He enjoyed malapropisms.

Susan

Leslie to Susan, December 18, 1983

Dear Susan,

Here in the compound is an ill-designed but well-equipped beauty salon. Walking from the hospital back to the apartment this evening, I stopped to pick up a few things at the market, which is in the same building, and on the way out noticed no customers in the salon and stopped in. The shop is moonlighted by a couple of young men from Bangladesh, and, for thirty riyals (3.45 riyals = $1), one agreed to cut my hair. Lacking clippers, he spent almost an hour trying to follow my instructions. Despite a ten-inch panatela and my most impressive scowl, he rendered my hair into something that Cary Grant might have worn in the fifties. A picture would be more informative; words will have to do.

One should move at least once every three years, lest the accumulation of the detritus of our past add weight to the inertia that impels us to continue in the old familiar ways. In sorting my worldly possessions into what to take and what to store, it was all too obvious that I had violated this maxim. The Albuquerque townhome was my longest single residence. It was not, however, an attempt to save transport or storage fees or to lighten the inertial load of my past that prompted me to return your letters. Now you are no longer free to mystify (fantasize) either me or our relationship, for your own words over this period of time create a picture far different from that which you are attempting to portray now.

After this last episode in our relationship, I intend in this letter to exercise my due and lay it on you. Having done so, I forswear any right to pass judgment on you ever more. Just as I was surprised, not at the fact of but at the extent of the detritus I

25

had collected, so am I to realize you are using yours to fabricate a cocoon of fuzz to insulate you from the real world. May the strength of my comments penetrate.

In the meanest surroundings, one may cultivate meaningful and rewarding relationships. From the poorest of soils, one may harvest a crop, but only in the absence of a choice is it commendable! You are fabricating a cocoon to convince yourself that you have no choice, that you are boxed in a canyon with no outlet, and that dying (death wish, the ultimate giving) from freezing (doesn't hurt as much when you are numbed) isn't all that bad. If you advance these arguments, you must also believe that it is better not to have loved, in order to avoid the risk of hurting, and you are also denying your own right to a place in the sun.

Read your letters.

You have indeed come a long way. From that shy, introverted adolescent, lacking in self-confidence to the beautiful (both inside and out) woman of promise that I once knew and cannot forget. But for whatever reasons, you now appear not only to have stopped evolving but are exhibiting definite symptoms of regression.

Stewart needs you, not worthy enough.

Stewart has his farm and will continue—with or without you. You are fantasizing, rationalizing your way to martyrdom.

I don't believe it, any of it. You are letting the cataracts of living too long in one small, incestuous place cloud your self-perception, your judgment. I don't believe you deceived me. Read your letters. I know the real Susan.

I have no wish to be an evangelist, to spread the word about the true path. I want to lead my own life. I want to share my life with you, day by day, in the real world. I am not flattered at the thought that you would rather have me a paper doll to ease the burden of your martyrdom than share your life with me. Yes, I am content, but I would willingly trade that for the happiness and pain of life with Susan.

I have heard your reasons for avoiding the fear and pain of divorcing Stewart, the only way to set each of you free, and I baldly state that they are a rationalization, an excuse to do nothing, not rock the boat, the easy way out. Read your letters. How can you come so far and not pay this final price?

Yes, I am angry with you, but better anger than disappointment. Despite your fears, your trepidation, let your love for me once more guide and help you. Let the pain that forces me now to tell you, *I need Susan,* add enough to your burdens to compel you to take this final step. The beauty that is Susan radiates, not unappreciated in North Dakota, but it is not enough. Let it glow at my side.

I have had my say. If the language is harsh, it matches my judgment, reflects the depth of my love. I will say no more.

Leslie

P.S. I lied. One more thing. If you doubt your own judgment, your own self-worth, you are wrong. You understood what I said in this letter! That alone refutes all of your arguments.

Susan to Sylvie, December 29, 2010

Dear Sylvie,

It took me days to write the attached response to your grandfather, to what I call his "final price" letter.

Initially, I told you why I married Stewart; he made me laugh. By the end of our fourteen years together, we rarely laughed, much less with one another. Even though I shoulder the blame for the demise of our marriage—because of my love for Leslie—I still believe that our marriage would have ended had I not met your grandfather.

Stewart is a good man; he eventually quit drinking and rented out the farm. He remarried nine years after we divorced. The year before our divorce, I asked him what he wanted out of life. His reply was to be happy. At the time, I thought it simplistic; now, I deem it admirable. May he have achieved what he wanted.

Happy New Year, Sylvie.

Susan

Susan to Leslie, January 17, 1984

Dear Leslie,

A martyr is "one who sacrifices his life or something of great value for the devotion to a cause." Always, I have been insecure. I shouldn't be. I do well without his physical presence. Think, think. I enjoyed my times best alone on the farm: no anger, no concerns about doing anything wrong—but, always, I had the emotional crutch. I grew up with him, the first man that never bored me. I can block out the negative, the mental abuse. Now I understand what you meant about humans being unique in their ability to forget. At the time you said that, I only wanted to remember what we shared. And I do, as I do the good times with Stewart. No one, most importantly myself, could fault me externally. I am a winner in that regard, as you told me to be. Internally, though, I failed. I am an emotional coward.

"How can you come so far and not pay this final price?" All the external possessions, the acceptance (or tolerance) of Stewart for me in curlers or any mundane circumstance, the known, the comfort of it. My whole world will shatter. I always wanted to be safe, sound, and secure, to belong. I am, I do, though I am a martyr whose cause is consuming me. Mentally, I know I am not sound and secure.

His abstinence from alcohol lasted two months—until the first fight. A very kind, different man he is without it. I have asked myself whether I would want to spend the rest of my life here, even if he did quit. My answer is still no. And, yes, he is a survivor. It has always been I who have run—and returned—in fear.

For almost ten years, I have wanted you. It began on the trip to Santa Barbara. And, yes, I have made you a paper doll. If I had stayed here, I would have kept the dream and the want of you in me until I died. Yes, to ease the pain of my martyrdom.

Your letter shocked me, Leslie, knowing me well enough to give me one last chance. After reading the letters and realizing the hurts I have inflicted upon you, I know that you should have told me to go to hell a long time ago. Read my letters. Yes, all there, all that my mind knows and my emotions have refuted.

I will take the final step and pay the price. I do not want to continue living for the sake of another. During the past three months, I have realized that we resent one another. I am not the person I used to be, what he wanted then and still does.

To do, to rock the boat. And, yes, I need you, too. I love you. Thank you for not forsaking me.

Susan

Susan checking the oil, summer 1976

A Courtship of Letters

Susan to Sylvie, January 2, 2011

Dear Sylvie,

In our few times alone, your grandfather and I exchanged words of love. The words, the memories, the hopes had been wrapped inside us for ten years. We were now free to unwrap and share our gift of love with one another. Leslie's word gifts were hand-printed on yellow legal paper; mine were typed on pilfered PCA letterhead. They crossed in the mail from North Dakota to Al Baha, Saudi Arabia. They are the physical treasures of my life.

By long day, I interviewed farmers and prepared taxes. It was my second year with PCA. I was a known and accepted entity in this very "man's world." As a farmer's wife, I knew the jargon and understood the perils and occasional monetary successes of this unpredictable avocation. It was a job that absorbed both my mind and more than the hours of each day. By short night, I planned, dreamed, and slept quickly. It was all I could do to keep the lid on the box of my joy, a joy I had not known I possessed.

More than a few tears have been shed rereading the attached letters, as I was transported back in memory to the beginning of the happiest time in my life.

Susan

Leslie to Susan, January 31, 1984

Dear Susan,

My own Saudi caper was intended to satisfy a multiplicity of needs, most of which appear achievable. I had some idea of what life in Arabia would be like and no great expectations for day-to-day living. All my surprises so far, and there have been many, have been most agreeable. We live in a compound attached to a 350-bed hospital, built and maintained to Western standards, with showers, potable water on tap, and air conditioning. Apartments are furnished, down to a complete kitchen and bed linens and there is cafeteria food with even a recently added pastry chef, who will be my undoing, just as I was getting my weight back under control. There is a staff of 1,100, of whom perhaps two hundred are Westerners (American, British, Australian, and Swedish), to satisfy social needs.

I have met others from different parts of the kingdom, and in comparing notes, I find that the expatriates here in Al Baha do indeed have it good. Al Baha won't be found on your maps of Arabia. On detailed ones, you may discover As Safir, its old name, roughly halfway between Jeddah, the largest city, on the Red Sea, and Abha, close to the Yemen border. At an elevation of 2,400 meters, the climate is close to idyllic ten out of twelve months. Only fifty kilometers from the Red Sea, there is an escarpment, just west of town, which drops off 1,500 meters most spectacularly and provides the meeting point between the moist tropical air of the sea and the desert highlands. Sunsets are of a dimension and color to satisfy the soul. Physically, the countryside resembles in vegetation and topography our own southwest. The Bedouin resemble in lifestyle the Navajo Indians, the villagers the Pueblo Indians. I feel much at home.

Perhaps as much as anything else, I appreciate my coworkers as conscientious and competent, the administration as quite professional. It is five years since I kept regular office hours and wore a coat and tie. It was difficult getting used to such a routine, but as the work becomes more demanding and I assume more responsibility, the old patterns reestablish themselves. The auditors arrive next week, and I am almost ready for them.

Yes, Susan, yes, yes, yes. Yes, you are a slow learner, but a good one. Yes, I believe you this time. I have always believed in you, but this time I also believe you. And yes, again for I know now what I didn't know in 1977, the power of your fears. This is one reason I returned your letters: to remind you of how much fear you have known and finally conquered. Yes, Susan, you can do it this time and, sweetest taste of all, you will have done it yourself. I want no other dowry.

Mail turnaround time is almost a month. Our letters will cross. I want this one in tomorrow's mail. For now, concentrate on what you must do. Keep in mind that you must join me as soon as possible, but you must come here as my legal wife.

My love for you is boundless. We shall have a honeymoon cruising the eastern Mediterranean, such as you cannot imagine. April and May are absolutely lovely in the Greek Isles. Keep that firmly in mind.

Leslie

Susan to Leslie, February 10, 1984

Dear Leslie,

It is terrible for a farmer to lose his hog barn and feeder pigs to a fire, have a taxable loss, and be told by his PCA assistant tax specialist that he has to pay $2,000 in recapture investment tax credit. The laws can be inequitable. I am now proficient in my work and thoroughly enjoy it. No longer is there needed a twenty-minute interval to penetrate the aloofness, which shielded my shyness.

The final telling is over, and the settlement is being digested. Hopefully, Stewart will give me an answer this weekend. When that is finalized, the lawyer said that it would take sixty days to complete the divorce.

To my surprise, I am doing and feeling all right. Obviously, the telling was painful and not what he wanted. I do think he realized that I would not stop this time when I presented the settlement to him. Stewart has not been cruel with words. He is still at the condo, but we rarely see one another and sleep in different rooms. I imagine he will soon leave.

Leslie, as I have not heard from you, I know I am doing this for myself. You are neither my crutch nor my escape. Thank you again for your letter, the return of mine, and what I learned about myself from reading them.

(The above was written in longhand late last night before your letter was received.)

One appointment after another and, in between, the office clerk handed me my mail. Excitement. I had to wait for two hours. Your faith in me has certainly been enduring, dear Leslie. You want me to be your wife, knowing I am not the same woman you loved nine years ago. As you have told me upon occasion, there is not just one special person for another. I have yet to find any other man but you I wanted to love and be with, and no one but you, where the sparks flew. May they still fly! Too much I have lived by the dictates of others. Are we rushing into something? We have wanted this for years, and the only thing stopping us was my fear. Yes, to your plans, whatever they may be for us.

How glad I am to know you like it there and are adapting to the requirements of your position, notably jacket and tie. It would be awful if you were unhappy. When you first told me you were going to Saudi Arabia, I could only picture a bleak, barren desert. My perceptions are confined to the wealth and abundance of the United States. I have been to Mexico twice and occasionally to Canada, which does not qualify me as a traveler. You asked last fall if I liked to travel. I do, but over the past few years, our trips have ended in miserable fights, clouding any enjoyment. When I did travel on my own, I enjoyed it. I have a lot to shrug off, and it will be done with welcome relief.

Did you enjoy your birthday? Do not be concerned about our age difference. I admire your wisdom, and I, too, now have an abundance of gray hair and character lines.

I feel so excited. I look behind me, and the work I have to complete is overwhelming. My job has been a blessing. Have not had a day off in weeks, but I do not mind.

After I read your letter, I took a short walk outside. Glorious day, 40 degrees, a February thaw, and I felt wonderful. I know I have read your other letter at least fifty times. Yes, your love for me has helped tremendously.

Despite my education and capabilities, I have not been adequately compensated. Perhaps someday, yet I would rather have the mental and emotional wealth without the confines of a nine-to-five job. Spoiled.

My thoughts are in a rush. Someday soon, we shall stand, hand in hand, overlooking the sea. A honeymoon, a real honeymoon, with you. Yes, yes, yes.

I have said it before, but I thank you for not giving up, for always believing in me. I love you, Leslie.

Susan

Leslie to Susan, February 4, 1984

Dear Susan,

Once, I think I wrote there are times when it is necessary to suspend belief, to take things on faith, the "Yes, Virginia, there is a Santa Claus" times in one's life. There is also a corollary to this: the times when it is necessary to suspend disbelief, the times when fear takes over.

There is nothing irrational about your fear. Everyone wants the security and comfort of familiarity that you express—wants it and needs it. The threat of loss can be terrifying. The known can be intolerable, but rarely so threatening as the fear of the unknown. There are many unpleasant ways to die, but none so horrible as the fear of dying. Fear is disbelief. Belief is the comfort of the known, the familiar. Willingness to venture out into the realm of the unknown is often the measure of the breadth of security base in the known. And you are about to shatter your security blanket! And for what? For some logical ideas about what you want out of life. For a life with a man who, no matter how much you love, you really only know intuitively! Not substantively! You must be out of your mind! Sound familiar?

Then, here we are. You are not out of your mind. You are right in doing what you must do. You do love me; intuitively is more than enough for now. We have plenty of time henceforth for the substance, and there is almost ten years to attest to the depth and reciprocity of that love. You have also the experience during those ten years of having faced your fears of the unknown and found them not only groundless but so rewarding for having faced them on your own and coming out a winner. How much of the comfort and pleasure you take from your life today is the consequence of having faced your fears? Remember your misgivings and fears when you considered returning to college? When you first arrived? Think of the fallout from that venture alone.

It really isn't true that all of your life so far has been a preamble, but you have repaid in full your bride price to Stewart. And, here it comes, you must now suspend your disbelief of what comes after. You must accept on faith that, just as your fondest hopes of what you expected college to give you have been vastly exceeded, so too your life when you have graduated from Stewart. Since you can't imagine, then you must take it on faith. No, Susan, there really isn't a Santa Claus, but there is a real Leslie. There is a Leslie, no paper doll, that is Susan's—and a Susan (hair curlers and all) that is Leslie's.

When I went to Beverly Hills last October to interview for this job, it was with the understanding that, some weeks later, after they had checked my references, they might make me an offer. Instead, they insisted on making an offer on the spot, allowing me only overnight to read the contract terms before pressing me to sign and leave almost immediately. It was only later that evening that I finally realized that that was the reason I had come for the interview in the first place. Why hesitate? And I didn't. I signed the next morning.

You have had a ten-year interview. It is time to sign.

You have lived fourteen years with Stewart. You grew up with him. He knows you, he tolerates you—your headaches, your silent sulks, your times in hair curlers. Did I mention your thing with toilet seats? I have lived with two daughters growing up, and if I don't know all the idiosyncrasies of Susan, I have managed to survive the growing-up process of daily life with them and managed to love them no less for the experience. I am prepared to suspend my belief in anticipation that daily life with Susan will also be rewarding. I am prepared to share not only the excitement of love but all of the experiences.

I envy Stewart the last five he shared with you. Comfort yourself, if this was a matter of concern. If you insist on worrying the point, give thought to how crusty a bachelor I may have become during this same time living alone!

Enough lecture. Trust me. I love you. Enough to have waited this long for you and let you do your own thing to prove yourself in your own way and without trying to crowd you. But now you are ready. Despite your fears, it is not me you must not fail; it is you.

In the mundane world, it is quite possible for you not only to join me but as a full employee with some rather remarkable benefits. Not only are salaries comparable to the states for US citizens, tax free, but so is your housing, and meals are subsidized. Excluding vacation, I can live quite comfortably on $500 a month. Since I am making $3,000, the rest goes into the bank. Even at my present salary, I expect to come back at the end of my contract with nearly $50,000 in cash. Between the two of us, we could bank a nice roll to start over in New Mexico.

Your first priority must be to start the clock running on the divorce in order to accelerate the earliest date when we can be legally married. I am not all that pressed for the legality of our commitment to each other, but the Saudis are real sticklers, as I will describe later.

You have paid your bride price to Stewart. I have earned your trust. Suspend your disbelief; do what you must do.

Leslie

Susan to Leslie, February 12, 1984

Dear Leslie,

No letter has ever given me as much pleasure and excitement as the one I received yesterday. Rare for me to be unable to sleep. It occurs when I am extremely excited, such as Christmas Eve, or very upset. Last night was the former. I like our yes, yes, yes. It was even hard for me to work today. I will pay for that tomorrow, will put in a longer day.

I would give much right now to be held by you, to share our love in words and with the passion that has never been satiated. If stats can be believed about women in their mid-thirties reaching their sexual peak, you had best conserve your strength.

Leslie, Leslie, I do know the time will pass quickly. I will not be afraid to love you. I have built a wall around me to shield my emotions, but the wall has to do with another man and what has now become a part of my past. Our love for each other and our being together shall crumble that wall.

As you in years past would say when I left in the spring, *au revoir.*

Susan

Leslie to Susan, February 5, 1984 (Leslie's birthday)

Dear Susan,

With mail taking a month turnaround time, our correspondence would be intolerably slow if we didn't abide crossing letters. Having spent such a protracted and intermittent courtship, one might expect that I had learned patience, but as our time finally draws near, the years of waiting pale, and I shall know many palpitations of anticipation these next few months.

A positive omen—your card mailed January 23 arrived today to touch me, your letter to warm me.

We know something about the compatibility of sex, our unique telepathic empathy, but all the little things, the cement of a relationship. Does he/she like garlic, get excited about Edith Piaf, toss in his/her sleep. What happens the first time he sees me eat a lemon? Whole? Yesterday I went out jeep exploring *wadis* with friends. We left at 9:00 a.m. and didn't get back until almost twelve hours later. Thoroughly delightful, my kind of weekend outing—and I thought of you constantly, wanting to share, to feel your vibrations. What if that's not your idea of how to spend your day off?

I have heard an argument favoring arranged marriages as being comparable to putting a kettle of cold water on a hot stove, love marriages as putting a kettle of boiling water on a cold stove. What happens when you put a kettle of boiling water on a hot stove? Even if we have had to arrange our own, it strikes me as a hot-on-hot set-up. If this reads as though my thoughts may be slipping over the edge a bit, maybe so. We have waited long enough. A bit of adrenalin, just to make sure it still turns on.

You may recall, for almost fifteen years, I was thirty-seven. I enjoyed every year of it and only somewhat hesitantly decided that, seven years ago, it was time to become fifty. Haven't had a moment's hesitation since. Fifty has been even better, and I figure that fifty is good for at least another eight or ten years. I enjoy my birthdays. Thank you for thinking of mine and letting me know it. I don't think an April has passed that I didn't think of you, but I don't ever remember wishing you happiness thereon. This year may be different.

Leslie

Susan to Leslie, February 15, 1984

My dear Leslie,

Will talk to you long before this arrives but I still need to write and for you to receive.

Your February 4 letter was given much thought by you to explain my fears to me. I have thought along the same lines lying in bed these past nights, but certainly not so eloquently stated. You are a marvelous conveyor of words, both written and spoken, one of your many admired qualities. Thank you for your contemplated acceptance of me in the day-to-day routine you will soon experience. You are right; I did not think about the other side: you. Somehow, I cannot perceive you as a crusty bachelor; as a matter of fact, I perceive your acquired talents as a bachelor as a plus (cooking, cleaning, dusting)!

Yes, what I have experienced with my initial fear and conquered is a great satisfaction to me, and I am very proud of some of my accomplishments. The length of time it has taken me to do what I am doing aside, I am satisfied with how I am handling the divorce proceedings and settlement.

I have not been upset emotionally. On the contrary, I am excited. I feel free. I have lived through the emotional hurts for a long time, the anguish for deciding—and I feel only relief.

Leslie, Leslie, patience for me and concentration on the pile of work behind me. I have to stop my thoughts about us until I crawl into bed at night.

The only physical evidence of stress is my weight loss, and I attribute that more to work. Sadly, to me, my chest goes first. I remember you once said your love for me was not measured by the cubic dimensions of my chest. The remembrance makes me smile.

The substance of each other—that, we shall learn. I am much more outgoing. I think you will like me more than you once did, do. My love for you has sustained me in more ways than I could relate over the last ten years. I can do nothing but look forward to a life spent with you, Leslie. At last, you shall become a known part of my life, not hidden.

Received one beautiful red rose for Valentine's Day, from the three young loan officers at PCA. The day ended reading your letter, the best of Valentine presents.

Susan

Leslie to Susan, February 10, 1984

Dear Susan,

Returned this evening at 7:30 p.m. from a weekend camping at the Red Sea. My second campout there, and equally enjoyable. Water temperature at 80 degrees, daytime perhaps 90 degrees, and overnight, not below 70 degrees this time of year. For a few winter months, it is most pleasant. Much too hot in summer. Water is clear. Coral reefs for snorkeling. Your letter waiting for me. What more could I ask for a lovely weekend finale?

We work, theoretically a forty-eight hour week, but in practice it is a forty-four hour week, starting on Saturday. Thursday and Friday are the weekend. The auditors should finish up their fieldwork this week, and routine should prevail for a while. Plenty to do, but I am not harried. Feel comfortable turning out competent work.

Don't be intimidated by my press to marry you. It is not to secure my commitment to you, but to make your life here more compatible.

What with passports and visa, both time-consuming, we shall have to plan pretty much in advance. I have some things in the works here with respect to employment for you that should be investigated further before you contact the hospital employer directly.

You are constantly in my thoughts. I would have it no other way.

Leslie

Susan to Leslie, February 17, 1984

My dear Leslie,

How wonderful it is to now love you freely in my mind. How many, many hours you, and the too few times we shared, have been thought about over the past years, a solace, a strength. I could never forget. Had I stayed on, it would have destroyed a part of me, the unreal paper doll to take out and examine.

I have told you I belong to you physically. I do. I have from the first time we shared our physical union, nine years ago. I never had the words to adequately tell you what it means to me. I still don't. It overwhelms me to this day that I should feel such freedom and abandonment in loving you physically and in the pleasures I gave and received. I never thought such an experience existed. You said we know somewhat of the compatibility of sex in your last letter. My, what we have to look forward to, to experience beyond the somewhat. I was never glad I was a woman until I was with you. I do know now I am striking, have never thought of myself as beautiful.

Birthdays are special to the Cash family. I am pleased you also enjoy yours. Unknown as to how it began, there is a tradition in the Cash family of rubbing butter on the birthday person's nose. Crazy, but we look forward to it. My dad is the applier. I was at my folks last April 3, expected it, but I was still caught unawares. Dad is laconic, tall, and handsome at sixty-six.

I have struggled successfully to overcome my silent tendencies, my irritability of inconsequential things, toilet lids notwithstanding. For years, I have learned to walk on eggshells in fear of doing or saying the wrong thing, unknowing what the wrong thing would be. I thought it was I, something wrong with me. I know my faults, know we will dispute, become annoyed with one another. Always, please, tell me why. I can and will accept a why but not a silent, unknown-of anger. It bewilders and hurts me. As you know the me of years past, though still inadequate at verbal expression, I am better. Until the end of Stewart and Susan, we never discussed the why of a fight. I relate this because it will accompany me, part of the "not rock the boat" that sank, and I don't want to repeat it. I rarely get mad, and if I do, it is usually over something foolish I did myself. Soul bearing, to disclose the last of my haunts.

Oh, Leslie, I just want to be content in all ways, I am socially, in my work, and that will go with me wherever I go. I give you now, after all these years, what I have never been able to give any man: both my mental and physical commitment.

Susan

Leslie to Susan, Valentine's Day 1984

Dear Susan,

Hopefully, we shall have talked together before you get this note, and it will be redundant, but while it is still fresh in my mind, I will put it in writing.

I had a profitable discussion yesterday with the personnel director and today with the finance director.

The best plan will be for us to find the right job opening for you, then have Beverly Hills sign you up and make all the arrangements to transport you here. Once this has been confirmed, I will meet you somewhere en route, perhaps Madrid. We shall be married and enjoy a brief honeymoon, and you will report for duty in Al Baha as Mrs. Freeman.

Moving right along, have I said I love you? Happy Valentine! The auditors should complete their fieldwork tomorrow, and, although they have been rather pleasant to work with (Arthur Andersen out of Jeddah), two Jordanians and one Saudi, they cannot help but be disruptive.

Three letters from you, the latest posted January 28—and none of mine, three at least, had reached you by then.

The love for you, which I have known all these years, grows impatient as our time comes closer. May your love and trust sustain you these next few weeks.

Leslie

Susan to Leslie, February 21, 1984

Dear Leslie,

Spring in February. It was 38 degrees when I left work tonight. The locals say we shall pay for the pleasure of such days come March. The worst blizzards in this area have occurred in March. Days will tell.

If you could see me now, you might change your mind! Hair curlers and dryer. Lloyd, our one-time neighbor, couldn't stop laughing for minutes when he saw me thus. He never let me forget either. Funny Lloyd, I think I wrote to you about him. My store of jokes I learned from him—and the ability to laugh at myself.

Last Saturday, I sat alone in my favorite farmhouse room. It was my last time to enjoy its peace and comfort, only I found it offered no comfort. It was no longer my home, and I felt no remorse in removing the articles I chose to take, forever destroying what once made it complete for me. As you told me when we spoke last Saturday, once I had made up my mind, experiences such as these would not bother me. That is not to say I could be a nomad, just that things of and by themselves do not constitute comfort or security. It is we who place such value upon things.

How reassuring it is to receive letters of love so often.

Susan

Leslie to Susan, February 22, 1984

Dear Susan,

The identification of large boobs with feminine sexuality is of quite recent vintage, starting with sweater girls during WWII, Howard Hughes's motion picture days (Jane Russell), and more or less culminating with Hugh Hefner and his competitors. Historically, feminine pulchritude has been associated with a bit of flesh, not the skinny models of recent years, but tits were only one item and all in proportion. The real measure: a graceful turn of limb, a slender neck, a bottom cupped neatly to the thigh, and firm, not pendulous mammaries.

Other than the typical American titillating fascination with the contents of a bra, I must confess that my attention is easily drawn to other anatomical aspects of the female form. When it comes to being sensuous, this comes strictly from within, as anyone who has ever formed his own opinion knows. Bewail not your loss of avoirdupois in boobs on my account. You have the beauty of proportion, and I know a sensuous woman when I meet her.

The chase has rarely tempted me. At least not since adolescent days. I find myself comfortable with monogamy and consider sexual relations integral to something more intimate in man/woman communications. I have known such intimacy with only four women in my life.

I have not known jealousy for thirty years and have given cause therefore only once. I cannot conceive of you ever providing me with cause and know intuitively that you know that of me.

You bubbled on the phone Sunday morning for what must have been a good hour, at horrible cost, but to my delight. And today, two of your letters (February 10, 12) arrived to fire my evening.

I care not what the world knows, only that Susan knows I love her.

Leslie

Can you imagine living with a man who writes like this?

Susan to Leslie, February 22, 1984

Dear Leslie,

I remember back to one of your occasional comments when we worked together. "Have I told you today how lovely you are?"

I never told you how overwhelmed I was by your presence those beginning years. You are everything I wanted in a man except for one minor detail, you are not tall. I use the past tense for I am recalling. Does your memory go back to the first time we went to Santa Barbara? It was then I realized I loved you, Leslie. The gift with no strings attached, you were wrong. When we had our first night and day together, those strings bound us until this very day. We only looked upon the gift given to one another. Now we shall open it and discover the wonder of what is inside.

Now very much in the present, I could never thank you enough for your patience.

Susan

Leslie to Susan, February 23, 1984

Dear Susan,

Jeddah, oldest, largest, most populous city (1.25 million), and diplomatic center of the Kingdom of Saudi Arabia, is hot and humid. Fifty kilometers south, there rises a high mountainous plateau that extends down into Yemen, and along its length, a narrow strip only a few kilometers wide, lies the only region in the peninsula where dry farming is possible and has been practiced for centuries. By the time you reach the summer capital of Taif, some two hundred kilometers south of Jeddah, the elevation is already at five thousand feet. The Al Baha region is another two hundred kilometers south and probably no more than seventy by forty kilometers in its greatest dimension. At seven thousand feet, it enjoys 400 mm (15.7 inches) of rain in a good year and is in the heartland of rural agriculture.

Nine years ago they saw their first passenger automobile. Today there are paved highways, and the Toyota Hilux pickup has replaced the camel. There is a current joke that prophesies giving superhighways to the Saudis is comparable to providing alcohol to the Indians. Genocide. All too prophetic. Like primitive agriculturists everywhere, these people are highly individualistic, fatalistic, shrewd bargainers, and ultra-fundamentalist conservatives. They are the rural Bible belt of Saudi Arabia.

Unused to the corrosive influence on their social customs of long exposure to expatriates, they fiercely guard their own practices and insist upon imposing them upon everyone. Male chauvinism is extreme by any standard and thoroughly institutionalized.

By custom and law, women are chattel, the personal property of their husbands or male relatives. Under special circumstances, they may hold title to realty and personal property but may not enter into contracts, drive cars, or have checking accounts. Their conduct and appearance in public is strictly regulated. They may not appear unless accompanied by their husband or close male relative and must be covered head to toe with an *abeya*, a loose-fitting black gown, their heads and faces veiled. Entertainment in the home, even among close friends, is strictly segregated. One must be related or extremely close to even inquire after the health of a man's female family members.

Expatriate women in public are excepted only the necessity of wearing the veil!

Life within the hospital and compound is a bit more relaxed but not much. Living quarters are segregated; social and physical contact between the sexes is quite limited. Fornication and homosexual acts are not only legal offenses but punishable in a fashion barbaric by any standards. The first week I was here, there was an attractive Filipino girl working in the payroll section who had earned a three-day weekend off. Mid-morning of her first day off, the finance director called me into his office to inform me that she had just been apprehended in the bedroom of one of the staff interpreters *in flagrante delicto*. Hospital administration was working to get her on a plane to Manila before nightfall to forestall her arrest by the religious police.

I am not trying to frighten you off. Seventy-five percent of the 1,100 employees are female, almost half are Westerners, to whom such conduct and social customs are ludicrously out of touch. Yet 90 percent successfully complete their contracts, no worse for the experience, and most manage to enjoy their tour. You will have no problem, but this background should increase your perspective as to my insistence upon our marriage—not that I needed any.

There are many things to admire and respect of the Saudis, but this is their country, and we are guests. Something like visiting Indian country in the Southwest, I do not find it onerous to observe their customs when visiting them.

Leslie

Susan to Leslie, February 29, 1984

My dear Leslie,

Thank you for your reassuring letter of February 22 regarding my anatomy. I also needed the uplift that your letter brought.

To live in a different world, even with restrictions I shall find confining and annoying at times, will be intriguing to me. I admit the restrictions entail more than I thought they would.

Enjoyed viewing the picture of the escarpment you sent, again amazed at my misconceptions of what the landscape is like. I never learned to play bridge. I have always enjoyed the nonthinking card games. Part of it has to do with the misconceived notion that an accountant is a whiz with numbers. It doesn't apply to me (such as being able to multiply and divide in my head). I champion progress; give me my calculator.

Tonight I was supposed to play racquetball, but my opponent has the flu. She is the number-one player, undefeated. The way I feel right now, I don't want to be defeated tonight.

My love for you will be more than I have been able to give to you in the past. I know that to be true.

Susan

Leslie to Susan, February 25, 1984

Dear Susan,

Ever since hearing of the capital of the Asir province, I have wanted to visit Abha/Khamis Mushayt, three hundred kilometers closer to the Yemen border and still on the *sahara* (highlands). Last weekend, two Finnish engineers and I went. Final decision wasn't made until late Wednesday night after bridge, and, since we both work half days on Thursday, we didn't get off until after 1:00 p.m. The drive wasn't eventful except for the descent and ascent of the escarpment, which is always delightful, particularly if you're not doing the driving. I really must get my license and help out on that score. The highway along the *tihama* (desert floor) is shorter, straighter, and faster.

We arrived at the hotel just before six o'clock and, seeking a parking spot, circumnavigated the building, whereupon I noticed, in a back room of the hotel, a girl unpacking what appeared to be good-sized paintings. Promising to investigate further, we hurried into the hotel to check in and, not waiting to unpack, out again to get to the *souk* (native market) before they started closing down. Fabulous. Street after street of shops and stalls, most everything available. Even saw frankincense and myrrh, both selling briskly.

Back to the hotel coffee shop for dinner at nine. Though not on the menu, convinced a cooperative and understanding *maître d'* to bring me a plate of assorted Mediterranean salads, *tabbouleh*, several hummus dishes, *kibbe*, and even a hot pepper. My companion's entrees were pale in comparison.

After coffee, we explored the back banquet rooms and discovered the girl I had seen, still unpacking large color photographs. I was prepared to leave until I noticed a few of the color prints and what appeared to be the photographer. I struck up a conversation that lasted until midnight. Delightful.

Tschekof Minosa spent two years living with the Arabs in and around Najran, a two-and-a-half-hour drive southeast, close to the Yemen border, won their confidence and obtained a series of photographs, unique and rare. After several months supervising the development and printing of his book, *Najran, Desert Garden of Arabia*, he was here to open his first showing in Khamis Mushayt. I departed with the first copy of his book, personally inscribed.

By hook or crook, I am going to get to Najran, but not without you. Hurry, hurry, hurry.

We spent the morning exploring the countryside and returned to the *souk* after a picnic lunch. I had been told of a rug merchant, whom we finally had found the night before, just as he was closing. The old man at the rug stall was gone, but the neatest young man, who easily out-manipulated my amateur attempts to bargain, sold me an old, used Yemeni camel saddlebag (hair, sand, and what distinctly appears to be camel shit firmly embedded in the tapestry).

We left at four, coming back along the *sahara* piddling along during daylight, hurrying when dark. Arrived at the apartment at 10:00 p.m. exhausted, exhilarated, and proud possessor of a used camel saddle bag, bread basket, and art book of photographs.

Leslie

Susan to Leslie, March 2, 1984

Dear Leslie,

As your weekend ends, mine begins. It is the first one I have had off in six weeks. First stop will be for strapping tape, brown paper, and packing materials, if I can find them. Best part of the weekend will be Saturday night, speaking with you.

It is beautiful today. When I went home for lunch, I changed into cords, casual shirt and sweater vest, and my dressy cowboy boots, discarding my silk blouse and skirt with the slit up the side. I feel much better.

My sister Christine and I have a strange sense of humor. She sent me the book *Unspeakable Acts,* from which I have been sending you cartoon copies. I think they are funny. I have been known to read funny cards in a shop and laugh until I cry, equally so reading touching Mother's Day cards. I am to discover that my sister has had the same experiences. When she bought *Unspeakable Acts,* she said a crowd gathered around her, enjoying her enjoying herself. Christine figures that the store sold quite a few copies because of her behavior.

Always, I warm to the different ways in which you tell me you love me, not using you but my name. The love I bear for you is not complete because it has so much more to give and learn and enjoy. Leslie, I wish I could hurry more.

Great line from a popular song: "If I said you had a beautiful body, would you hold it against me?"

Susan

Leslie to Susan, March 3, 1984

Dear Susan,

Payday is monthly, on the fifth. The traumas of producing 1,100 paychecks on inadequate data processing equipment are not diminished for being only monthly instead of more frequent. Night before last, the father of our payroll chief suffered a paralyzing stroke. Yesterday morning, the payroll chief left to join his family in Amman, Jordan. Yesterday and today, I worked, absent phone calls and other interruptions. Working on the weekend is tranquil, but inadequate compensation for having to work.

Last night, I could no longer deny my hunger for some good old chile. Some time ago, I discovered not only a can of pinto beans, but a four-ounce can of honest-to-god green chiles. Stopping by the hospital kitchen on the way to the apartment, I picked up fresh onions, garlic, and even a couple of green onions for garnish. With forethought, I had brought several packets of red chile powder with me from Albuquerque. Cooking for one is not my idea of cooking, but for a couple of hours, the aroma in the apartment was compensation enough. Substituting hamburger for pork shoulder, the end result was not only edible, but my gut glowed satisfactorily for a couple of hours afterward. *Molto contento.*

Only worked until noon today and, after a nap, propped up two legs of the dining room table to finish a drawing sketched on the beach at the Red Sea some weeks ago. Within the hour, the sky clouded over and we enjoyed a real thundershower, hail and all. Neighbors rushing about in the storm to get photos of snow in Arabia! About as much sense as trying to use natural light to draw by in a thunderstorm. I ended up doing household chores, necessary but a waste of a weekend at home.

Your February 17 letter and resume arrived yesterday. Will start circulating the resume tomorrow. Will reread your letter often.

The freedom to love without restraint, without guilt, without reserve within the deep-seated comfort and knowledge that however expressed, it is welcomed as openly and unreservedly by the beloved. Not only the apogee of physical union, the fleeting glimpse of a smile inward directed, the knowledge of a shared reaction, a glance of recognition, the casual touch that electrifies, intuitive, nonverbal sharing. Pleasure enhanced, magnified for being shared not for being secret. This to me is the uniqueness of love. The bond between a man and woman— but the bond needs exposure to become binding.

Yes, Susan, I knew long ago that you were mine, and for me there would never be another Susan. And I was frightened. I knew what needed to be done. I opened the door to my own private Pandora's box that I might taste, confirm what I already knew. And the box, once opened, cannot be closed again. Three times have I tried. The fear was not for me. I already knew I had the confidence that the reward was worth the price. If I wasn't convinced you also had that deep-seated self-confidence, I could not have persevered. That is what I meant when I told you to be a winner. You already were a winner, but you didn't know. Others have told you the same. Now you know it also, and that, dear Susan, is the difference. With such knowledge, it is possible to be content. With each other, we will know happiness.

I weary of the literature communion. I long for the nonverbal.

Leslie

Susan to Leslie, March 3, 1984

My dear Leslie,

This is written after we talked, the time before court decrees and an upsetting week. The cost be damned, for I need you in voice, as I cannot have your physical presence now. Oh, Leslie, I know we shall have a rich life together.

When I was fifteen, I was befriended by a woman named Esther. She gave me a gift that has brought many rewards to my life. She never knew of this gift. She died twelve years ago, and with her unexpected death, I felt my first anguish of loss for a person I loved. What hurt most was that I never told her I loved her or how much she meant to me. To honor her memory, I vowed to always relate to others what I perceive to be special about them, even if it is seemingly insignificant.

The past three years I have failed. I have lost some of my sensitivity. I find it is returning. I have built a wall around myself to not hurt. You understood this in your December letter, a letter that shook me, haunted me, one line more than any other: "How can you come so far and not pay this final price?" No one knows more than I the price I paid. No blame to Stewart.

Would I still choose to remain if I had never received your letter? I cannot honestly answer the question, only after receiving it and understanding what you meant, I would leave whether you would be in my life or not. Of that I am sure. In time, I think I shall understand and appreciate what others see in me, the best of me, which I do not see in myself.

This may sound silly, but during the worst of times the past few years, the inner me says it is okay, I love you, go on and be the winner you have fought to become. I do like myself, Leslie, have never wanted or desired to be anyone other than myself.

My last month of waiting will be enjoyable. A week with my sister, then on to California with time for my folks and friends, with the heightened anticipation of soon. At last, at last, the time for us. My love and trust for you does sustain me.

Susan

Leslie to Susan, March 5, 1984—Payday

Dear Susan,

There are only two things I enjoy doing in bed; reading and writing are not among them. It is just after 8:00 p.m., and I have turned down offers to play tennis and bridge. Freshly showered and shampooed (no curlers), slightly paunchy, with a bowl of chile, I look forward to an evening "at home," the pleasure of writing to you, and the prospect of reading, which, like my drawing in Arabia, languishes from disuse.

Long days in the office recently. I don't particularly mind, but it tends to interfere with other activities in which I would rather indulge.

You sounded almost normal on the phone Sunday. The more I read and hear from you, the more I want to know about this Susan. I knew a little about an earlier version. The later version sounds even better.

Some time ago, while still with our former employer, I went to visit our labor attorney in Century City. The receptionist took me down a long hall and, as we passed an open office door, I looked in and, amazed, recognized the occupant as someone I had not seen in years. Just as he looked up, I exclaimed, "My god."

Just as quickly, and with a deadpan expression, he replied, "You mistake me for my father!"

This comes to mind when I think that, collectively, we have lived some eighty-five years with very little for shared experiences. Over the next eighty-five, we will build our own and possibly re-create some of the former in discovering each other's families and friends.

Howsomever, I am just as pleased that life is a one-way path. There is little in my past I would ever wish to retread, as much as I may have enjoyed it. Friendships strengthen with time but not with absence, and those that have lapsed with distance have been replaced with new. Those that we have known separately will undoubtedly grow when we share them in twain (in twain?). I look forward to meeting yours, for if you found attachment in them, they would also be my kind of people.

One serious drawback to this apartment is the lack of decent chairs to read in; writing and eating are well accommodated. Reading is not. So I sit in my bed to read. And so to bed.

Leslie

Susan to Leslie, March 7, 1984

Dear Leslie,

Driving west at 7:00 p.m., I marveled at the expanse of the Dakota plains, awesome in its desolation. Magnificent sunset as far as I could see, nothing to block its beauty. The Red River valley, the choicest soil in the United States, home to dedicated farmers—many wealthy, many more who barely eke out a living. They love farming and the earth. I do admire them.

I sat in a courtroom this day and answered the presented twenty questions. The lawyer and I had rehearsed them beforehand. I thought a lot about my answers afterward and changed some. He told me later it was the only time he had ever listened to the answers. For once in my life, Leslie, I was eloquent in spoken word. It was important I did so this day. I do not marry you with the thought "if it doesn't work out, we can be divorced." I knew when I married Stewart I felt no passion. It was based on our friendship. He is the only friend I have ever lost.

We have the passion, the mental telepathy that has bound us for years. We have yet to discover the depths of friendship in its truest sense. I know it is there. If I didn't, I would not marry you, Leslie.

On my desk this morning was a red, long-stemmed rose with a note, "Hang in there."

My last letter was very self-centered. You write of things, except closing paragraphs, and I write of feelings, a male/female difference perhaps. Others see in me what I do not. Yes, the insulation not to be what I am. It is ripped off. I am proud of how I have acted. This month has aged me with lack of sleep and stress. I do feel good this night, a finality. I am basically patient, but once I set my mind to a course of action, I want it finalized immediately. I hated "we'll sees" as a child.

The you I know, have dreamed about for nine years, your hands, their touch on me, your words, the essence of your person, has lived in me. I know you always would, your understanding of the paper doll theory.

You, more than I, will feel the difference in our ages. My fault it took so long. I believe our time together will be rich. I won't adore you. I have done so. I will love you for the man you are.

I offer to you freely, after all these years, Susan, a person you know but do not know.

Susan

Leslie to Susan, March 13, 1984

(Sylvie, when Leslie had a momentary lapse of memory for a name, he would call either your mother, your aunt, or myself, George. In this instance, he is addressing someone impersonally. Pedal hypothermia? Cold feet.)

Dear George,

Pedal hypothermia—I must be crazy to think of marriage again. You've got it made as a bachelor, self-supporting, even enjoy your own cooking and are a competent housekeeper.

Middle-aged women find you attractive, hearts flutter as you pass. You come and go as you please.

You have watched her grow over the years and marvel to see her blossom, but will she grow on, right past you? Ah, but you have been a part of her as she has grown. Both feeding and guiding her—and you are already a part of her. See how she stands on her own feet, not too steady yet, but that will come. She no longer needs you. That is how far she has come.

She is a man's woman. There are few men that could ever satisfy her, and you are one. And if she no longer needs you, she loves you, and wants you. Most men can only dream of such a woman, and if by chance they should discover such a one, would not even recognize her. But you know. Yes, you know. As strong and independent as you are now, so will she be soon enough without you. There is a lock on each of our futures, the key to which lies in the other's possession. Fool! Do you lack the courage of your own knowledge? Mock your intuition? Have you not seen over the wall? The moment so long awaited has come. Take this woman, your woman, to wife!

Life as a bachelor may be a high calorie diet, but bread alone does not satisfy. Classic symptom of a protein deficient diet is pedal hypothermia.

The above was written (and sent) to let you know that the pompous, overbearingly confident exterior has its converse side.

No mail for almost a week. Today four letters with enclosures written between February 27 and March 4. My cup runneth over. I shall savor them yet a while.

Moments, emotions, often vivid, do I recall of Susan and Leslie, but dates rarely (what can you expect of a man who sometimes forgets even the names of his children?). The events and impressions of that March day in 1975 are surely a part of us, but lacking your memory, the date is not. Sitting on a hill, mud on our shoes, overlooking the San Joaquin Valley in clear midmorning light, holding Susan in my arms, vibrant with a love unripened as yet, without even a kiss, and of such promise and future as I was expectant and fearful of exploring. Riding to and from Gorman, holding hands for the first time in a bar over a martini. We even tried to dance once! But don't ask me what color your eyes, how tall.

We are both squares in a world with few corners left, naive if not inexperienced. But possessed of a common knowledge of what is right and a deep intuitive knowledge of each other, confirmed by our love. What in hell more could we ask.

Pedal hypothermia be damned. We belong to each other, lock, keys, and all. I love you.

Leslie

Susan to Leslie, March 21, 1984

Dear Leslie,

I marvel at us and our belief in one another. We are to marry, have not seen one another in over three years, and have only the rudiments of friendship. Yes, I had pedal hypothermia, too, Leslie. I have never been on my own, first tied to the dictates of parent/child then husband/wife. I use the word dictates; both "guardians" have given me freedoms, it was I who imposed the limitations. I made the mistake of molding myself into what another man wanted. Unfair to each of us by the time I realized it.

I have met men I liked the past ten years, been flattered, made binding friendships with some, but there was always you in me. You describe it well, the lock and key. I would always feel cheated if I did not know what life was like with Leslie in its fullest sense.

Had you lived still in Albuquerque, progression would have been slower. Suspend my disbelief, I have. Yet, I must also be realistic. I write of, remember, the passion; I want more for us. I know of only a few truly happy marriages among my friends.

They have passion for one another; it is clearly evident even after fifteen years of marriage.

The walls I have built around me will not come down overnight. I will try, especially in anger. I will love you for the man you are and not expect you to be all things to me. More importantly, not to freeze in anger and expect what I have known the past years. I realize I have recounted this before, these feelings give me cold feet more than anything else.

George. You haven't addressed me by that name in years. I smiled when I read it. Mr. Freeman and George.

Susan

Leslie to Susan, March 26, 1984

Dear Susan,

Typical, I'm afraid, of the difference between us is the fact that, like you, there hasn't been an April since I have known (1975?) when I have not thought of you and us, but unlike your timely message to me, this one will reach you after the fact. May the celebration thereof have been of joyous note to all who shared it with you.

Despite all its golden merit, silence is poor substitute for the right word at the right moment. I still smart for my ineptitude last Sunday morning in failing to remind us, that despite the mood of the moment, we should be rejoicing for we are already joined together. Susan and Leslie in bonds committed in love nine years ago that have now grown so that only space and a short time longer separates us, both of minor import considering the challenges already met. Our union is no less strong for lack of daily consummation, will not be strengthened in legal bonds of matrimony. It exists because we are free to commit and pledge what we already know. Viscerally, intuitively, rationally, Susan belongs to Leslie. Leslie belongs to Susan. Our physical union will serve to enhance, enrich our union, not bind it.

Surely there is sufficient comfort in this knowledge to carry us through these last few days and uncertainties of the moment.

Characteristically, surely not a symptom of senescence, for my memory has always been imperfect, I cannot recreate either the conditions surrounding our relationship nor the specific sentiments of the moment for each of those nine years, but with a certainty my thoughts were of Susan and the "what if" of any future for us conceivable at the time. My thoughts, for many years now, have been invariably directed to the future, the past only involuntarily. In contemplating your 1984 birthday, it is not the past nine (or thirty-six) that entertain me, but the next nine (or thirty-six) and how/where we shall celebrate them. The burden of April 3, 1984, without Susan is lightened in the knowledge that it will be the last.

Let the promise of our future sustain us through uncertainties of the moment. Happy Birthday to Susan.

Is that butter on your nose?

Leslie

Susan to Leslie, April 17, 1984

My dear Leslie,

So long we have waited. You rationally, I in dreams. No matter now, for it is past. Forgive me this morning; you shall learn your wife is slow to show excitement. It took an hour for it all to sink in. Unfair to you, I think now, but know I shall compensate. Still lacking in verbal expression, whereas you are so proficient.

I have loved you for almost ten years. Five days to wait after all these years. All our romantic planning is secondary. I want only to be with you. The words I should have said this morning.

We shall utter a few words for legalities without the pomp and circumstance of youth and firsts. Know that I belong to you in a totality I never have experienced with another person.

I know you forgive me for the pain I have caused in growing up. The now and our future, our reward, especially mine.

We shall know laughter; our own shared experiences and understanding of one another, in time told with a knowing glance; infrequent anger, learned to be discussed; and, perhaps, in time satiate, for only the time, the passion we have for one another.

My darling Leslie, words I have never said to you and so much more held in reserve. Yes, you hold the key to unlock that reserve.

Susan

Susan to Sylvie, January 6, 2011

Dear Sylvie,

The "dweller in my endless dreams" walked down a corridor in the Los Angeles International Airport (LAX) on April 22, 1984. We spent the next two days in a hotel room, emerging for food and covering up when the hotel maid changed out the towels. On the third day, Leslie perused the yellow pages, making calls until he found a minister who would marry us that evening. Reverend O'Connor happily informed him the flowers were still fresh from the Sunday service. With only we three in attendance, Leslie Francis Freeman wed Emily Susan Cash on April 25, 1984.

The best part of my life had just begun.

Susan

The picture we sent from Al Baha announcing our marriage

Arabia

Susan to Sylvie, January 10, 2011

Dear Sylvie,

Before marrying your grandfather, my worldly travels consisted of a winter outing to the Winnipeg Zoo when I was in college and a day in the Ensenada, Mexico, police station, even though I had proof of Mexican auto insurance. My first passport was filled with stamps, little patches showing my hopscotching around the world. The first of my travels with Leslie was unique: King Fahad Hospital, Al Baha, Saudi Arabia.

Not wanting to forget my initial impressions, I maintained a journal of my thoughts and experiences. Attached are my 1984 entries.

Susan

Susan's Journal, 1984

<u>6 May 1984</u>

Thirty hours after departing LAX, we landed in Jeddah, Saudi Arabia's largest city, located on the west coast of the kingdom, by the Red Sea. We spent the night at the Red Sea Palace; such opulence I didn't expect. Collapsed around 1:00 a.m. and quickly awakened by the call to prayer before first light. Early morning was already hot and muggy as we strolled through Jeddah's main *souk*.

On my first day of school in a foreign country, with Leslie as my teacher, a group of Al Baha employees rode through the city, strewn with construction sites, on the Blue Bird, a yellow bus transporting us on the six-hour trek to King Fahad Hospital. Saudi Arabia has been in a state of modernization the past eleven years due to the enormous wealth generated by petrol dollars. Per capita income is $7,000. Leslie informed me that the ministry grants loans for new buildings—both home and business. The loans need not be repaid until the building is complete. Consequently, nothing is ever complete, with steel spikes glistening on the roof tops. He joked that the unofficial state bird of Arabia is the steel crane.

Leaving the desert dust of construction, the scenery changed to glimpses of centuries past with grazing goats, sheep, and camels. In the distance was the occasional Bedu camp. The Bedouins are nomadic Arabs who have lived in tents and shepherded their flocks of sheep and herds of camels for centuries. From the desert floor, we ascended the escarpment, some seven thousand feet, stopping in Taif, the king's summer capital, for lunch. The kingdom was organized into its present state in 1932, with King Fahad being the fifth of the modern rulers. One of his four wives is from the Baha region, and it has flourished from his good favor.

King Fahad Hospital was built in 1979; it had three hundred and fifty beds, eleven hundred employees and was operated by American Medical International (AMI) under contract to the Ministry of Health. The hospital complex, situated on the highest land level in Baha, was an impressive first sight. The employees referred to it as the hill. It is not unlike a college campus with its many apartments, recreational buildings, tennis courts, warehouse, and the hospital itself. Housing was provided at no charge. Meal tickets were $2.00—free for those earning less than $10,000 annually.

<u>10 May 1984</u>

For my first trip to the Al Baha *souk*, I was properly attired in a borrowed black *abeya*. We had purchased one that evening for 20 Saudi riyals (1 riyal = 35 cents). AMI buses ran on a regular schedule from the hospital to Al Baha. The *souk* merchants operated specialty shops, each merchandising one particular ware. I thought that my favorite was going to be the bread bakery located in a back alley of the *souk*. Fruits, vegetables, and dates were sold on the streets. Pork and alcohol were forbidden, and fresh milk was unavailable.

<u>12 May 1984</u>

A group of us drove down the other side of the escarpment, a hair-raising ride on a narrow road best suited for four-wheel drive vehicles. We set up our borrowed tent by the Red Sea. It was the clearest water I had ever seen. I walked out twenty feet to a coral reef and viewed an array of exotic fish. Snorkeling and spear fishing were popular sports. Some of those exotic fish were later speared and provided a feast, roasted in foil with Greek salads, Arabic flat bread, fruit, and espresso for dessert. We were a mix of Swedes, Greeks, Italians, and Americans. With no Saudis present, we endured the muggy heat conditions in our swimsuits. After sunset, I had my initial experience skinny-dipping with Leslie. One could not help but feel the Biblical history as we walked along the shore, even though the sea didn't part.

<u>20 May 1984</u>

Leslie is playing bridge tonight. I won't attempt to learn, as we need some separate activities. He is proficient at whatever he does. I have heard he is one of the best tennis players in the complex as well as bridge players. He is a good cook, also, and does his share of the domestics. Nice.

24 May 1984—Thursday afternoon, weekend begins

A few hours alone before Leslie arrives. Realized I was upset but did not know why. My first time of being sharp with Leslie. Later, we went swimming and, with wet hair, he took me to bed and asked what was troubling me.

He already reads me better than I do him. Shuddering shadows, memories on which the door does not close. I could not tell him.

25 May 1984

Leslie decided we would spend the day alone. He remembered it was our one month anniversary and prepared brunch. In the quiet moments of being held, I could talk about the shadows. We have both agreed to open ourselves to one another, as difficult as that might be, especially for him. He told me that, for all the changes I have undergone and the emotional high of the past months, I was bound to experience a letdown. He was surprised it hadn't occurred sooner.

We spent the evening listening to *La Boehme* and learning to dance together. I realize it has struck; the known of the past nine years built in North Dakota is gone. This is the present, only a little known even of Leslie.

Take heart; you are far stronger than you realize. Leslie's last words to me this day: "I love you, Mrs. F."

27 May 1984

Work is getting busier, and I enjoy it. Not unlike what I did years ago at Bio-Medical: mediator and problem solver with my added ability of being well-ordered.

The discrimination against third-country nationals (TCN's) is abhorrent to me. Seelan, my assistant, approximately thirty-seven, is a Sri Lankan. Sri Lanka, formerly Ceylon, is a small country off the tip of India. He is not an AMI employee but subcontracted through an Arabian company. Though his employer was paid $8,840 per annum, Seelan receives less than half, which he remitted to his wife and two children. When I arrived, he had been here two-plus years, and he is an excellent, conscientious worker.

There was a hierarchy, with the privileged Westerners on top, then Egyptians and Jordanians, Filipinos, Sri Lankans, and the bottom rung—Bangladeshis. One did not cross the lines. From the Filipinos down, they were deferential and polite. I wondered how much hidden resentment there was. I tried to be cheerful and polite to them all.

As an example of some of the inequities, if a Westerner were summoned home due to the death or serious illness of a family member, AMI granted paid leave and round-trip airfare. The Filipinos received ten days paid leave, no airfare. The Marcos regime required AMI to submit 70 percent of the Filipinos' salary to a relative back home.

In our tiny apartment, designated for one Westerner, they would house four Filipinos. Leslie says that, in our travels, we shall see a lot of poverty and discrimination. How sheltered I have been.

8 June 1984

Ramadan, the Muslim period of fasting, has begun. Muslims are not allowed to eat, drink, smoke, or have sexual relations during daylight hours; nor are non-Muslims allowed the same activities in the presence of Muslims. To do so means immediate deportation. The windows of the cafeteria are whited-out to accommodate the non-Muslim staff.

14 June 1984

We took an evening trip to the *souk*. Buses run only at night during Ramadan, when the Muslims break their fast. After a bit of successful shopping—a zipper for me, an Arabic journal to record checks, and tennis balls for Leslie—we went to a Turkish restaurant at 10:00 p.m. for dinner. We invited two Egyptian physicians to join us. As Arabic is Egypt's native tongue, they ordered a sampling of most of the restaurant's entrees. We began with Moussy, a nonalcoholic Swiss beer; flat bread; cut tomatoes; and cucumbers with hot peppers. The main course consisted of lamb kebabs; a mini pizza with ground mutton and spices; long rolls of ground meat deliciously seasoned; boiled mutton, which I do not like; barbecued chicken; and, for dessert, baklava and Turkish coffee. Have yet to drink Arabic coffee made from a green bean with cardamom. Turkish coffee is dense; the grounds form a thick sediment. We were asked if we wanted light, medium, or heavy, which refers to the amount of sweetening. I chose medium and enjoyed it. The conversation was entertaining, as the two Egyptians are true expatriates, well-traveled, practicing in different countries as a career. They both speak four languages: Arabic, English, French, and Italian. We missed the last bus at midnight, as we stopped and bought Leslie's favorites: an assortment of Arabic cookies, a quarter-kilo of baklava, and flat bread. We shared a taxi for the return trip. It was a pleasant night, nice to get out. Today was also the anniversary of the occasion of our meeting one another, eleven years ago.

15 June 1984

Friday, the last day of the weekend, Leslie napped, and I walked to the northern perimeter. Sat on a rock by the fence and observed a wild desert plant in bloom; it resembled the puffballs growing in the ditches by the farm. North Dakota *had* become home. I felt lonely and bewildered. Thought how self-centered I was. Reminded myself I could not embellish the life I had in North Dakota or my life with Stewart. Realized I needed to cultivate more acquaintances.

It is not good to be alone when I feel like this. I went home and read *Saudi Arabia, An Artist's View of the Past*. The prints are lovely, capturing traditions lost to progress and oil megabucks during the past fifty years.

18 June 1984

Nursing Administration, my department, with a total staff of approximately four hundred, was not only blessed to have Seelan but Jessie, our secretary and typist. Jessie was a Filipino male, probably early forties, even-tempered, and the ears and eyes of the Filipino community. Anything I needed to know about the Filipino community, I asked Jessie. Thus, I asked him about someone who could hem and put a zipper in a skirt I had purchased in the Baha *souk*. It had three metallic gold leaves hanging from the waistband! It was returned within two days.

Part of my job entailed leave request processing for our department, home or annual leave days. Requests had to be submitted sixty days in advance. Westerners got a total of fifty-one leave days a year, Filipinos thirty days, Sri Lankans fifteen days. Filipinos and Sri Lankans worked six days a week and we, five and a half. For emergency leaves, I could process the paper work in a few hours and have them on a plane in two days, as time was needed to procure an exit/reentry visa.

MaLou was a Filipino nurse whose father died, and she was my first emergency leave. She returned this week, stopped in the office to thank me for my help, and presented me with a cream, embroidered lace blouse. Overwhelmed. It is even more touching and a true gift of sacrifice when you consider how little they are paid. After the required 70 percent is sent home, they are left with little spending money.

Wore the new blouse today, and Jessie told me, "Ma'am you look even more beautiful today." People stopped me in the hall, commenting on the blouse. I did enjoy the attention.

This has been my sixth week and the roughest emotionally. Have struggled not to think about Stewart, wondering how he is, being stunned after all this time that I divorced him, married

Leslie, and live in Saudi Arabia! Others have told me the sixth week is the worst. Came home to find a letter from one of my North Dakota friends. Her words of love and friendship snapped the mood. Relief, for my feelings this past week scared me, as did my seeming lack of control over them. Did not want to share them with Leslie and realized it affected my physical closeness with him, as of course, did he.

27 June 1984

Invited to the executive director's villa for a *bon voyage* party. The villa was built on the highest ledge of the hill, commanding a panoramic view from the third-floor terrace. Looking down at the complex, I was reminded once again of the haves and have-nots. Wore my Filipino blouse and a new, long, black embroidered skirt I bought from a Filipino nurse. Leslie often tells me I am the best-looking woman on the compound. I'll wear this outfit in the States. Sampled food treats of celery and chocolate-covered strawberries.

With Leslie's compliments this evening, I thought of Stewart. The last years, there were few, if any, compliments. Perhaps it was also true on my part. It is easier to realize and understand all the tensions and problems with time. Sometimes it hurts a lot, but at least I am becoming more realistic.

Seelan shared pictures he received from home, home being Colombo, Sri Lanka, of his daughter's coming-of-age celebration in Hindu tradition. She appeared to be a lovely young girl dressed in an Indian silk sarong. Seelan said her costume is not unlike what she will wear when she weds. I was pleased that he shared them with me. Seelan may be cast as a have-not, but he has more inside than anyone else I have met here.

26 July 1984

Work has been hectic, often quite frustrating of late, for both Seelan and me. Yesterday, I told Seelan about a poster I had seen. "It is hard to soar with eagles when you work with a bunch of turkeys." How he laughed.

Though I met Jean, the assistant director of nursing, when I first arrived, only recently have we begun to enjoy each other's sense of humor. The other day, we were discussing AMI's policy of giving us thirty days' additional storage of our goods at home after we terminate our employment. She said that, knowing AMI, her things are probably with Joe's Store and Haul. The extra thirty days gives Joe time to call back her goods, which he has rented out. Advertised with rental of a personal touch, "family heirlooms available."

We'll have another Trivial Pursuit party after Leslie and I move to our two-bedroom apartment. I asked Jean if she had ever played it. She has. Said she cheats, though, even cheats at Monopoly and did so over the years playing with her kids. She added that they grew up to be persons who did not cheat. I said, "No wonder; they didn't want to grow up and be like their mom." Our banter is fun and always occurs when I need a laugh at work. She leaves in February, has been here almost three years.

Gold is plentiful in Arabia, probably the cheapest prices in the world. Jean wears a large gold link-chain bracelet, which I commented upon. Her retort, "vulgar, isn't it?"

My one and only gold possession is from Leslie, my wedding gift, a unique tricolor bracelet. We have tried to find a matching band. As he is not possessive, I find it humorous that he wants me to be marked as married. Even outside the compound and wearing the black *abeya*, I am conscious of being stared at by men. At first, I thought it was just because I was a Western woman, but Leslie said no, it was due to my striking appearance. How nice to be so complimented.

<u>3 August 1984—Goat Grab</u>

Most Westerners hope during their tenure at King Fahad Hospital to be invited to an Arabic home. Fifteen of us were extended such an invitation to a wealthy Baha villa. The house commands an impressive view of Mt. Ibriheim, the largest mountain in Saudi Arabia, and of the remains of the original stone village and watchtower. The surrounding hills are terraced with small fields, formed with rock barriers, that have been cultivated for centuries. Most farming ceased during the seventies, with the advent of petrodollars. The watchtowers were defensive shelters from invading Turks.

The entrance, steps, and frontal portion of the home were covered with polished marble slabs. We removed our shoes upon entering and were ushered into a large room lit by four impressive chandeliers. The only furnishings were colorful floor bolsters and a wall unit housing a television. Seated on the floor, we were offered dates and almonds, accompanied by Arabic coffee, a strong brew flavored with cardamom seeds, the odor and taste of which I shall never forget. After an introduction to the male members of the family, most of whom spoke excellent English, the children were presented. Arabic women are not seen in a mixed group. The women of our group were invited to their quarters. None of them spoke English, but we communicated with gestures and our combined knowledge of Arabic expressing our thanks, complimenting their children and home. Sixteen extended family members reside in the villa.

After we had played games with the children, a pickup arrived with a black sheep. Muslims only eat meat that has been slaughtered and bled the same day. We, as their guests, were led to the back of the house to watch as two Egyptian servants expertly slit the throat, decapitated, and skinned the main course. Most of us took pictures, a rarity, for the majority of Arabs will not allow pictures to be taken. After this display, we were again seated upon a carpet spread on the marble porch and offered a Moussy. Few could drink it after what we had witnessed.

Several hours later, we were ushered inside to the dining room. A large piece of plastic covered the carpet, on which were placed bowls of oranges, grapes, and peaches. The grapes and peaches had been grown by our host on his two farms. Neither plates nor utensils were used. As a concession to us, we were offered plates. Again, we sat on the floor, and I participated in my first goat grab—on this day, lamb. The boiled lamb was served atop rice on two large platters, decorated with the entrails. Had this been served to me in the United States, I would have immediately thrown up.

Muslims eat only with their right hands. The left hand is considered unclean, as it is used to wipe oneself after elimination. It is the reason the right hand is amputated for thieves; never again are they allowed to eat in the company of others. Keeping this in mind, we all grabbed pieces of lamb off the bone with our right hands, alternating with portions of rice. One of our hosts noticed that I was having difficulty ripping the meat off with my hand, as it was hot. He politely pulled off pieces of meat and tossed them onto my plate, along with the liver. I later learned it is an honor to be served the liver. Unfortunately, I don't consider eating liver an honor. Leslie tactfully ate it.

The day before my first goat grab, Leslie and I had been invited to the curry kitchen, a separate cafeteria operated by AMI for the Sri Lankan and Bangladesh hospital employees. Curry, to them, simply means spice—not the powder we associate with the term. They use chile powder as we do salt and pepper. The menu included fish curry, dal, rice, and salad. Fish curry was good, but it was the dal, a hot, spicy lentil dish, I enjoyed, providing yet another taste treat.

Part of the unique experience of living here is eating all different kinds of food. Despite occasional bouts of Baha revenge, my food preferences have expanded.

Goat Grab, Al Baha, Saudi Arabia

<u>6 September 1984—Airborne somewhere over the</u>
<u>Mediterranean Sea</u>

The five pillars of Islam are as follows: (1) the unitarian nature of Allah, (2) giving alms to those less fortunate, (3) praying five times a day, (4) fasting from sunup to sundown during Ramadan, and (5) performing the Hajj, a pilgrimage at least once to Mecca during a Muslim's lifetime.

Ramadan occurred during June. Both Ramadan and Hajj begin according to specific lunar sightings. In our modern times, if it is a cloudy night close to the beginning of their month, they send up a jet! This year, over 1.5 million Muslims made the pilgrimage to Mecca from all over the world. Non-Muslims are forbidden in Mecca. On the expressway to Jeddah from Al Baha, the turnoff for Mecca is clearly marked "Muslims only." Non-Muslims refer to the other highway as the Christian bypass. The airport at Jeddah has impressive campgrounds for the pilgrims, providing shelter for the Hajjis with tent-like cement domes.

The Hajj is occurring now, and, in a few days, there will be a mass country exodus. When we arrived at the airport this morning, there were relatively few travelers, and the employees were all pleasant, far different from my initial arrival in the kingdom. Sheer accident, as we never thought about Hajj, though I doubt many Muslims live in Rome.

Flying on an L10-11, at thirty-six still the thrill, I have slept a total of ten to eleven hours the past two nights, Christmas in September. Leslie is taking his second nap; he hates to fly. As we are flying Saudi Airlines, I am wearing a long dress and *abeya*, though I observe that some of the other women are not. Tomorrow I will probably be wearing shorts in public, as it was 90 degrees in Rome two days ago. How strange that will feel. I like the absence of alcohol. Though I shall enjoy a glass of Italian wine, I relish the thought of ham and ice cream even more.

When I stop and think about all the places we shall see, I am overwhelmed. Working with the nurses and management staff in my department and processing their leave requests, I have become accustomed to "Destination" being almost anyplace one could imagine.

<u>14 October 1984</u>

AMI is cutting back on salaries and benefits. Concerned over losing a three-year contract bid that we won't know about until spring. If they do lose the contract, AMI will be out of business on August 10, 1985. Everyone is tense. Constant change and upheaval is the realm of our work lives.

I met a female Lloyd. She told me that my appearance was that of a refined lady until she got to know the other side of me one night at a barbecue. Unfortunately for us, we discovered each other too late. She left two weeks ago, and it was my first experience of watching the Wednesday-night bus depart with tears on my cheeks. I and a host of others watched Michigan Maggie depart. She left her mark on many lives. She wants the inscription on her tombstone to read, "She made them laugh, even when they didn't want to." Next departures will be Seelan in January and Jean in February.

Leslie continues to be kind and understanding, never gets mad at me, only becomes frustrated when I retreat inside, which I am still prone to doing. Thought I would be better by now. Spoke once with Jean about it. She was divorced ten years ago, her choice, and she said it takes a long, long time to get over it, especially with all that has changed for me. To me, she is well adjusted psychologically.

19 October 1985

This is my weekend night, off tomorrow and Friday, and on my walk home, I wished I was home. It was part farm thought and part unknown home in Albuquerque, so I could bake bread or go shopping or watch TV or drive. The thoughts passed once I entered the apartment. Hopefully, I will remain appreciative of the many freedoms we as US citizens possess.

These longings were probably prompted by the events of the day. As my boss was off, I was instructed by the personnel director to fire one of our nurses. She had been caught in a male apartment building. Nothing was transpiring. She had been informed-on to the security guards. Western society would dub it entrapment. Irrespective that no immoral act had occurred, a single woman is forbidden to be in the company of a man without the presence of a married couple. Had it not been the weekend, he and she both would have been on a plane tomorrow. To add to the excitement, three of our administrative department heads—one is the executive director of the hospital—were driving to Jeddah yesterday, were involved in a car accident, and were placed in jail. All parties involved in auto accidents are assumed guilty, and, if not injured or dead, are imprisoned, generally only for a brief time. There are only interim days of dullness at King Fahad Hospital.

Speaking of the king, his majesty is scheduled to visit his namesake in the next two weeks. Drat, he doesn't want to see any women; even the floors chosen to be graced by his presence have instructions for the nurses to absent themselves. Incredible, 1984, and his word is law. The hospital and Baha have benefited, though, by the completion of the highway from the hospital to Baha in honor of the visit.

Leslie told me I would be a different person in six months. The time nears. I don't think I am, at least not dramatically changed.

<u>5 November 1984</u>

Leslie thinks that we build up flora and fauna in our guts to stave off the occasional bug or critter we unwittingly ingest. I don't think the Western flora and fauna we brought with us to Al Baha are a match for the Arabian bugs. Leslie and I drove friends to Jeddah preceding their three-week leave, and we had a memorable dinner at one of Jeddah's finest restaurants. I had my first—and last—culinary experience with grape leaves.

Am now in bed, have been in and out of it the past week and a half. At first, I assumed it was Baha revenge. Employee Health gave me some meds to stop the horrible cramps and diarrhea. The diarrhea continued, and I started excreting tissue from the intestinal walls. After a series of tests, they diagnosed the microorganism doing me in. It is highly contagious and can be fatal if untreated. How exciting to have a communicable disease, Shigella (the g should be a t). I am now taking copious amounts of pills. If not better today, they will hospitalize me. My opinion of that is totally negative. Already, the cramps are subsiding. It is a terrible way to lose weight. It is also depressing lying in bed, feeling rotten. Read a good book, though, *In the Footsteps of a Camel*, about an American family working for ARAMCO (Arabian American Oil Company, the first

American company in the kingdom) who took frequent treks to the eastern part of Arabia in the early sixties. The book contains exceptional pictures and stories about Bedouin life.

Received a humorous letter from Michigan Maggie today. Quote: "needless to say, I am very glad to be home. I look back on Saudi as a learning experience I am glad I had, but the knowledge that I have the freedom to drive a car, show cleavage, and drink in public without the fear of imprisonment or deportation is *wonderful.*"

6 November 1984—Observations of Saudi customs as I expel the last of those damn bugs

By Western standards, women are second-class citizens in Saudi Arabia. We Western women must adhere to their customs, and neither they nor we are allowed to drive. If a Saudi woman is seen in the clinics or hospitalized, only a male member of her family can decide whether a tooth can be filled or an operation performed. Men and women are forbidden to touch in public. A man cannot address a woman unless she is his wife or a member of his extended family. A woman can only be seen in public accompanied by her husband, a married couple, or a member of her extended family. Marriages are arranged, and by the words of the Prophet Mohammed, a man may have as many as four wives, as long as he treats them equally. Once, this would have meant an equal tent for each wife. Today, the increased wealth and price of urban dwelling renders it too expensive for most Saudi men to afford more than one wife.

It is interesting to hear conversations others have had with Saudi women who lived for a while in the United States. Usually, these women are wives of men who finish their graduate studies in our country and return to Saudi to begin their own business. Many women find their customs too restrictive upon returning. Some did not like their husbands freely talking to other women and were glad to return. Whatever their feelings, tradition and respect for the wishes of their families supersede their own personal desires.

On our first trip to Jeddah, Leslie and I decided to see the city via bus rather than taxi. As we attempted to board, all the men and the driver were pointing to the rear of the bus. A fifth of the seating area is sealed off with a separate entry for women only. I sat alone in the back, truly conscious for the first time of what segregation feels like. It feels like second-class.

With all the restrictions on women and the behavior between men and women, I am still taken aback by observing two men walking, talking, and holding hands. Men have a very formal and structured method of greeting, not only in what they say but in shaking hands and kissing one another on the cheek several times. It is not very reassuring to see two large Somali hospital security guards holding hands.

If a person is convicted of murder, rape, sodomy, drug trafficking, or armed robbery, he or she is publicly beheaded. If one is convicted of stealing, the right hand is publicly amputated. Within the past twenty years, the custom was still to hang the severed member, head or hand, on the main gate of the city. Three years ago, in Baha, a Saudi man was publicly decapitated. He had spent the prior ten years imprisoned, accused of murdering a man. The murdered Saudi had a young son. It was the son's decision, upon coming of age, to determine the form and degree of punishment. Tough to wait ten years to lose one's head.

Because of the severity of Muslim penalties, AMI deals swiftly with infractions of Saudi customs by employees—before the Baha religious police can intervene. Within a single week, five British and Filipino employees were sent home for fraternizing with members of the opposite sex. It does not matter how innocent one is, if a female is caught visiting in a male building or vice versa, it's time to pack for home.

One of the five pillars of Islam is praying five times a day to Allah. Before tape recorders and loud speakers, the *muezzin* would call the faithful to prayer with his chants from the mosque. All shops in the *souk* must close for prayer, be they here in Baha or the metropolitan city of Jeddah. The shopkeepers are not required to attend the mosque but are required to close during the twenty minutes or so for prayer time. The chant was eerie at first, but I have grown to like it. There is a separate mosque adjacent to the hospital. We can hear the calls from our apartment in the predawn and late-evening hours. Through the loudspeaker system in the hospital, we hear the prayer calls during the day. It is impossible to hold a conversation during the chant. On each of the seven hospital floors, large prayer rugs are provided, facing Mecca, on which the faithful kneel and pray to Allah. Women are not allowed in the mosques, but as faithful Muslims they, too, pray five times a day.

Sylvie to Susan, January 17, 2011

Dear Susan,

I've enjoyed reading about your life in the hospital compound, and you have provided me with a better understanding of Muslim practices. But I don't think I could deal with all the restrictions you describe. I would like to see the Middle East, though. I remember you and Grandpa enjoyed your trips to Turkey.

Sylvie

Susan to Sylvie, January 25, 2011

Dear Sylvie,

Turkey is my second-favorite country, probably because the topography is similar to New Mexico with the added splendor of the Mediterranean. The Turks consider themselves European rather than Asian, even though 97 percent of their land mass resides on the Asian continent.

My next attachment details our trip to Kenya in January of 1985. For years, I had a picture on my desk of an airborne hot-air balloon, perfectly fitting for a resident of Albuquerque, the balloon capital of the world. Only this picture was taken drifting over the Serengeti Plains, and I was a happy speck in the basket. Africa. A safari in Kenya with a finale leg in Sana'a, Yemen, ranks as one of our best trips.

Susan

Susan's Journal, 1985

January 1985—Kenya

Kenya, formerly part of British East Africa, gained its independence in 1963, after the tumultuous and bloody Mau Mau Uprising. Probably to the surprise of Kenya's liberators, it has grown with a viable economy and is the only politically stable African country. Its largest source of revenue is tourism, which surpassed coffee two years ago.

Nairobi, at the height of summer, was a lush, green paradise after months in Arabia, with jacaranda and flame trees just coming into bloom. We stayed at the New Stanley Hotel, famed for its Thorn Tree Café, where the great white hunters of yesteryear pinned notes to the tree trunk for their fellow safari companions. We were a compatible tour group of three: Leslie, myself, and Diane, one of the head nurses from the hospital—and our Kikuyu driver/guide, James.

Traveling in a Nissan diesel van with a lift-up top for game viewing, we headed north from Nairobi, through rolling hills planted with maize and coffee. Our first destination was Nanyuki, site of the Mt. Kenya Safari Club. Mt. Kenya loomed in the distance, its peak blanketed with clouds. We spent the night at the famed club, where one must dress for dinner; the fireplace in our rooms was a luxurious beginning to the equally enjoyable lodges and tents in which we were to spend our nights. Having arranged accommodations with full board on the safari, we found that the lodges served excellent breakfasts and lunch buffets, each having a set menu for dinner. We enjoyed Kenyan Tusker's beer, but not the papaya wine, and satiated our desire for pork.

Descending from the highlands and the Mt. Kenya area into the Great Rift Valley, we viewed our first wildlife: impalas, Thompson's Gazelle, baboons, and warthogs. In the distance, thousands of flamingos rimmed the perimeter of the soda bed lake with their fuchsia hue. The best game viewing was in the Masai Mara Reserve. Greeted at the park entrance by Masai women, cousins to the Watusi, we were more intrigued by their earlobes than the bead work they were selling. One tall, slender woman had a plastic 35 mm film container inserted in her lower lobe.

Our tents were situated on an elevated bank where we witnessed an evening parade of animals, including a bull elephant, congregating within a hundred feet of us for their evening drink. Our first morning in Masai Mara, we came upon six lionesses who had just brought down a zebra. We stopped within twenty feet, joining a herd of cape buffalo on one side and the more fortunate zebra members on the other. With the zebra still alive, the lionesses began eating its hindquarters. A jolting reminder this was not Lion Country Safari Land. In time, the lionesses made a circle around the cape buffalo and returned with their cubs. James told us they hide the cubs before a kill and sometimes forget where they left them. That's when the cape buffalo take over. We saw giraffes, three black rhinos, hippos, hartebeest, wildebeest, and exotic birds.

Early on the second morning, Leslie and Diane waved good-bye as I ascended in a hot air balloon with six others for an idyllic one-hour ride. We floated at wind speed, rising to 2,500 feet, and drifting back to bird level, ignored by the wildlife below. Perfect landing; the ground crew hacked down a small area of wild grass, unrolled a canvas, and we sat on empty butane tanks to enjoy a champagne and chicken brunch.

Our last stop was Amboseli Park, the first established game reserve in Kenya. Ample snow melt from Mt. Kilimanjaro affords a year-round water supply. We saw lots of baby elephants—one no more than a week old. James told us that, during droughts, the female will not produce. Sitting around the campfire, one of the staff members told us that a guest in 1976 was killed in his tent by a lion. Subsequently, they had built the lodge, and, six months ago, installed an electric fence around the perimeter. We did not venture to ask about intervening causalities.

Susan to Sylvie, January 28, 2011

Dear Sylvie,

Whatever was to happen between AMI and the Ministry of Health over contract negotiations, Leslie and I, and many others, decided to end our employment in August 1985. We began saving and planning for our last and best adventure, a six-week train trip beginning in London and terminating in Hong Kong.

Our last months were chaotic, preparing to leave, bidding farewell to transitory friends we would never see again, dealing with shortages, and the unique problems one faced working at King Fahad Hospital. Days before we departed, my favorite hospital memo was issued:

To: All head nurses or charge nurses
From: Cart room supervisor
Date: 5 August 1985
Subject: Cotton balls—RECALL

It has been brought to my attention the current supply of cotton balls obtained from Al Baha to cover the period awaiting delivery from our regular supplier is infested with fleas. It is therefore recommended all stock of such nonsterile cotton balls be removed from carts and destroyed immediately. Since sterilization of the cotton balls will not remove the fleas, there will no longer be any cotton balls available until the warehouse is able to supply us. I hope this does not cause too much inconvenience for you and your staff.

Our Masalama (good-bye) Party, King Fahad Hospital, August, 1985

We departed Al Baha on August 16, our last trip on the yellow Blue Bird. From Jeddah, we flew to London, sightseeing for a few days before boarding a bus to Glasgow.

I don't think of myself as a whiner, but I did remark at a London eatery that the orange juice was tepid. When we arrived at our hotel in Glasgow, I complained about the tiny bedroom with the meter box requiring coins for heat (reachable by inching around the bed sideways). Upon hearing this last comment, Leslie, in his calm and didactic manner, informed me that our six-week train trip would not be pleasant if I continually found fault with the food and rooms. The delights of travel are the discoveries found in what one sees and experiences, not in what one eats or where one sleeps. My feelings were hurt, and I reverted to my learned adversarial behavior. Thus, we spent the next several days in unaccustomed silence, and when we arrived in Inverness, I sought solace on the bank of the River Ness, crying and eventually resolving to heed his advice. Our first fight upset us both. Leslie, who had quit smoking his pipe for almost a year, resumed his nicotine intake.

After a week in Scotland, we returned to London and grandly embarked upon our six-week tour with a champagne breakfast at Grosvenor Hotel. Our first train ride terminated in Folkestone, and we departed England via ferry to Boulogne, France. We traveled by train but spent nights in Paris, West Berlin, and Moscow as we transversed the land mass of Europe.

As I was transcribing my journal entries, I consulted the Internet for a more detailed description of a place we visited in Mongolia and discovered that anyone could take a train trip as we did—via YouTube! What was once exotic to me is now, if not commonplace, easily viewed on the Web or any number of cable shows. Thus, I won't attach my daily journal entries save one, Shanghai, to give you a flavor of what we experienced.

Susan

Susan's Journal 1985—Central Kingdom Express

<u>29 September–2 October 1985, Peace Hotel, Shanghai</u>

The Peace Hotel, formerly the Cathay, was built by the British in the thirties, located on the Bund, and, in its day a first-class, renowned hotel. Now run by the Chinese, it is in good repair and loaded with charm. Coffee is served in fifty-year-old silver pots. We have stayed in excellent new hotels, crummy new hotels with intermittent hot water and leaking toilets, and unusual guesthouses. So much for hotels. They do become important after five weeks of traveling and an overnight on the train, sans suitcase. The suitcases traveled separately, as there were four of us in a Chinese sleeping compartment. Our compartment partners had as much hand baggage as we used for all our luggage.

When we began our tour, guide Melissa told us about some of her former tours: the lady brandishing a knife whenever anyone entered her train compartment on the four-day trek across Siberia, people hospitalized along the way, one of whom died. She finished her summary with the statement that no complete group had ever made it to Hong Kong. I finally commented that we must seem a dull, boring bunch. She dryly replied, "Wait until the fifth week; people can take most things for three to four weeks and be polite. During the last weeks, their true colors are flown." Melissa never embellished, she was always forthright in what we could anticipate, and occasionally painted such a bleak outlook that we were thrilled when it was better than described.

We are now in the last week, and the woman to whom everything was "wonderful, wonderful," I have heard utter several nasty comments. Two single women roommates have not spoken to one another for the past week. One tour member said if she heard George say, "very nice" again, she would scream. Still, I think we are an amicable group. Fortunately, our worst mishaps occurred in the first week and not the last. Everyone has been sick at least once. Three had to see a physician in Nanjing; two will only eat rice, as they are sick of Chinese food.

One does not find Western food except in first-class hotels and only in southern China. Then there are the Freemans who eat and try everything. We even go out on the streets and buy interesting foodstuff from local village vendors. For fare the others will not try, they now say, "give it to the Freemans; they'll eat it." Obviously, our girth has not decreased. I must admit I, too, am tiring of Chinese food. I long for green salads, green chile burritos, and milk. The Chinese do not consume dairy products. At meals, they serve either a choice of sugared fruit drinks or beer. We have learned to check the bottle for the occasional fly or other bug body before drinking. In first-class hotels they add the choice of mineral water, which I have learned to gag down, as I rarely drink the beer. It is good beer, but after all the time of not drinking, I prefer only the rare glass. Hot tea is not served. Chinese custom is to drink tea between meals, tepid rather than hot. And as in Europe, beverages are served at room temperature, not chilled.

October 1 is National Day. This year celebrates thirty-six years of independence for the People's Republic of China. Shanghai's main thoroughfare, Nanjing Road, prohibited vehicles from 6:30 to 11:30 p.m. The buildings were decorated with lights, and it was enjoyable to walk, hand in hand, with the crowd. We were the anomalies moving in a mass of Oriental humanity. Leslie observed a small child observing us. He tugged on his mother's sleeve. Capturing her attention, he pointed at us and with his index finger, pulled up the corner of his eye.

We spent the afternoon on a three-and–a-half-hour cruise, sitting in deck chairs viewing one of the largest, busiest harbors in the world. We have visited a commune and seen the Shanghai Acrobatics and a Chinese folklore concert.

Susan to Sylvie, January 31, 2011

Dear Sylvie,

During our six-week tour, not once did I complain about what I ate or where I slept. Only twice did I decline an unusual foodstuff: a gelatinous duck web soup and a thousand-year-old egg that smelled like sulfur.

Aside from being the trip of a lifetime in where we went and what we experienced, our six weeks in close proximity cemented our relationship. In one of his premarital letters, Leslie described the uniqueness of love: the fleeting glimpse of a smile inward directed, the knowledge of a shared reaction, a glance of recognition, and our intuitive, nonverbal sharing. All of these enhance and magnify one's pleasure in the other.

In Moscow, our group was assigned an Intourist guide. She informed us that we must follow her at all times. Leslie and I spoke not a word and quietly left the group to explore on our own. Walking along Moscow's side streets, peering in storefronts with few if any goods, we observed shoppers queuing in long lines (we were sternly lectured upon our return). The glance of recognition that passed between us as we watched the Chinese child explain with a hand motion we had different eyes. Without being asked, the loving gesture of Leslie filling pitcher after pitcher with water in a Chinese guesthouse to rinse my long hair on a night when I was too ill to take a shower or bath. And without complaining on my part, we walked mile after mile in Shanghai to find pipe tobacco. I found it for him in the Number One Department Store—Panda Tobacco. Leslie said it tasted just like its name.

Of note, we were the first of Melissa's groups to make it intact to Hong Kong.

Our year and a half honeymoon was over. We retouched American soil in Hawaii, spending a few days with our safari friend Diane. New Mexico was our final destination. Though others have thought it foreign, it does not require a passport for entry.

Susan

Camel ride on the Mongolian grasslands, September, 1985

Letters from the Land of Enchantment

Susan to Sylvie, February 1, 2011

Dear Sylvie,

Emerging from the cocoon encasing us in Arabia, we stepped back into the Western world, eventually arriving in Albuquerque on November 1, 1985. Within a few months, we were both employed and spent the weekends exploring our enchanted state.

We still wrote the occasional letter to one another. Leslie returned to creating his meticulous pencil drawings and maintaining written contact with family and friends. His letters imparted bits of wisdom interspersed with humor. They were generic in nature, sometimes topical, sometimes descriptive of a trip, and in all ways, welcome missives from Leslie the wordsmith.

Leslie once said he wrote to entertain himself. Putting his thoughts into writing forced him to organize, within the structural bounds of composition, those random ideas drifting across the haze between conscious and subconscious.

He often copied a cartoon from *The New Yorker* magazine into his letter, reproduced without benefit of their knowledge, much less their consent. One hopes that, if they knew, he would be forgiven (not sued), with his subscription spanning almost fifty years with brief interludes for army duty and time in Saudi Arabia. The cartoon originally copied onto the attached letter was entitled "Caller IQ." It depicted a matron holding a phone receiver as she gazes on the digital printout next to the phone, "your husband, 112." Copies of all his generic letters, some longhand but most created with the computer, pilfered cartoons included, are housed in a notebook which will also become yours.

Susan

Leslie's Letter, 1995

SCAT

Scat, n. the unassimilated end product of the animal digestive process. Feces. From Ancient Visigothic sh*t into Old German which added the 'c' before the 'h' (Germans cannot stand to leave an 'h' stand by itself), directly into Mod.E without the benefit of the purgatorial fires of M.E. Where the Brits aspirated the 'h' dropped the 'ih' sound for the 'ah' retaining the consonant 't', (a place to stop the tongue from protruding out beyond the teeth). - **ology** the study of scat. - **ological** adj., frequently used to describe the British sense of Musical Hall humor. - **ologist,** one who studies scat. (A proper British Mum would never admit to an offspring who studied sh*t for a living, but would boast of a son/daughter who was a scatologist secure in the knowledge her uninformed listener was ignorantly impressed.)

I am no scatologist, do not even pretend to any particular interest therein, but anyone who has survived the age of twelve has accumulated an inventory of personal scatological anecdotes sufficient to qualify one as knowledgeable if not expert.

For example, even the casually observant would note the droppings of herbivores is typically spheroidal or pancake in form; the carnivore, turdoidal elongate; and the omnivore, depending upon its diet over the past forty-eight hours, something in between. And that territorially defensive predators exhibit an inordinate interest in the scat of other species, including and especially that of other members of their own species, discovered on their turf. One need only observe the olfactory objects of compulsive interest to dogs in the neighborhood.

On the western approach to the delightful small town of Moab, on the Colorado River in the deeply eroded canyon country of southeastern Utah, there is a sprawling, architecturally modest rock shop, owned and operated by a noted amateur archaeologist, offering a fabulous assortment of both mineral and fossil artifacts. Along one aisle is a row of perhaps half a dozen white porcelain commodes, sans seats and water tanks, filled with what appear to be spherical black rocks the size of golf balls. The hand lettered sign indicates "Dinosaur Turds 25 cents each," herbivore species, obviously.

Intrepid travelers with no particular interest in the subject, often, in fact, acute distaste, are constantly exposed to its variances. Not only the impact of different diets on one's own digestive system, but in particular, the means offered for disposing of the end product. Any woman exposed to an "Eastern" toilet can so readily attest. Consider squatting over a hole in the dirty metal floor of a unisex compartment in a moving train, attempting to maintain balance with a firm grip on a hand rail with one hand, attempting to restrain your garments from dragging on the floor with the other, and performing! Susan told me that her first try on a Chinese train ended in a draw.

Tour guides at the Grecian-Roman ruins of Ephesus make a point of highlighting the Crapatorium, a four-sided, roofless structure whose marbled interior is adorned with a marble bench on three sides, cut-out in a recognizable utilitarian format, comfortably accommodating up to thirty sociable participants at any one time over an irrigation canal concealed under the bench. Well, why not? They had public baths, didn't they?

Sana'a, the capital of Yemen, has a number of large, multistoried townhouses of ancient vintage, constructed of timber, stone, and mud, with characteristically striking exteriors. Most attractive. We were fortunate enough to tour the interior of one, which we were assured was typical. In the same corner of each story, we discovered their version of a crapatorium, consisting of a relatively small, perhaps eight to ten feet square, enclosed room with a tiled floor tilted toward the outermost corner, which had a hole, ten to twelve inches in diameter, the topmost opening of a closed chase leading straight down to a deep pit beneath the building foundation. Care, of course, had to be taken, in the process of construction, to ensure that each separate chase was properly arranged and plumb, for the protection and comfort of any temporary occupant of the floors below. Otherwise unadorned, the room was furnished with a water jug; toilet paper is an unknown, even to this day. Ecologically thrifty, the pit was periodically harvested of its desiccated lower contents for use as fertilizer, thereby extending the life of the reservoir.

From 1945 until the early 1980s, tourism was not encouraged in mainland China; hospitality facilities were badly neglected. In the eighties, as the country was opened up to visitors, hotels and restaurants were being built in a rush to fill the void. Lacking resources of their own, the Chinese government had contracted with international hotel chains to fill the gap—with the caveat that all construction be done with local labor. Lodged on an upper floor of a brand-new hotel in Beijing (formerly Peking) in 1985, we overlooked the construction site of another multistoried hotel. Ours was less than a year old and, though not world-class, conformed to contemporary international standards. Already a bit shabby, everything seemed to work properly, except for the toilet that leaked copiously around the base of the commode when flushed. Talking to other members of our tour group, we discovered the problem was common in all rooms.

Next to the bank of elevators on our floor was an oversize set of double doors. Seeing them ajar as I was going down to breakfast the first morning and waiting for the elevator, I peeked in. It opened directly upon a common chase with plumbing, HVAC, and electrical conduit rising, unhindered, the height of the building. In addition to the conduit, there was a veritable waterfall raining down, starting at the top floor and increasing in flow at each successive descending floor.

Puzzling? Puffing on my pipe and casually watching the workmen on the construction site from our truncated balcony, while waiting for Susan to finish her morning ablutions, I noticed the workmen uncrating toilets. Each crate contained a modern, one-piece commode, seat and lid, a plastic bag of hardware, and a gasket seal, all packed in excelsior. The workmen removed the contents, carefully saved the crate wood, and pitched the excelsior and gasket seals into an untidy smoldering pile.

Puzzling? And then upon me it dawned. The pieces of the puzzle fell into place. The Chinese laborers, unfamiliar with Western plumbing fixtures, failed to recognize the essential nature of the gasket seal for installation. Lacking ring gasket seals, toilets leak.

During the 1930s, when Chiang was fighting both the Japanese and Communists in China, an elderly Chinese man, listening to Pearl Buck extoll the virtues of modern Western plumbing, wondered about the values of a society which considered it an improvement in living standards by moving the outhouse inside the home.

Leslie

Susan to Sylvie, February 5, 2011

Dear Sylvie,

You might not remember, but February 5 was your grandfather's birthday. The last one we shared together was nine years ago. The card I gave him depicted two birds in a cage singing to one another, and inside, the caption read, "I will never finish loving you." And I haven't.

More memories of him, not contained in our letters, floated through my mind this day. In our eighteen years of marriage, I witnessed one burst of his anger and the use of the f word, as he slammed the front door and walked out, conceding momentary defeat to a computer. There were annoyances caused by me. I am a finicky fish consumer. I must have complained about the bones or too raw or too something one evening. Leslie got up from the table, took my plate to the kitchen, sat back down, and continued eating his meal—without uttering a word. I left, went upstairs, and cried. Almost daily compliments, he was ever chivalrous, even to holding my chair at our own table. He told me that he decided as a young man that, if he could not attract girls with his great wit, charm, or brains, he would be the most chivalrous of the male contenders.

Attached is one of my letters to Leslie. Our letters became celebratory in nature, marked by dates. We were not consistent. Some years I might get a Valentine or a birthday card or an anniversary letter. One Valentine's Day, a lunch-size, brown paper bag was left on my pillow with a drawn heart, inscribed LFF loves ESF. It, along with the letters, resides in my box of treasures.

Susan

Susan to Leslie, March 18, 1987

Dear Leslie,

You would not remember, as I do, this date, twelve years ago, our first time together, our day and a night, and I was never the same.

I wanted a crystal ball before I decided to leave North Dakota. Not in my wildest dreams could I have envisioned our past three years. At that point, I think I would have been unable to comprehend the depth of love we now share. I told you once that I did not think I was capable of loving someone as much as I do you.

In three years the bad: some lost teeth, two scars, a few times of anger, less gum, more wrinkles, and less hair for each. In three years the good—it would take pages.

Give us this day and our tomorrows to add to those pages.

Susan

Sylvie to Susan, February 10, 2011

Dear Susan,

I didn't remember Grandpa's birthday. I do remember making him cards as I grew up, just not the date.

When you wrote about Grandpa removing your plate from the table—Mom has the same memory from her childhood. I think she cried too.

Sylvie

Susan to Sylvie, February 15, 2011

Dear Sylvie,

It has been enjoyable to read again Leslie's many letters. One of my favorites is the attached *Bread* letter.

I also have another box that contains every card you made and sent to us on birthdays and Christmas and thank you notes. I'll return these to you when the size of your apartment expands.

Susan

Leslie's Letter, 1994

BREAD

In the winter of 1942-43, our family moved to Flushing, Long Island, in the borough of Queens, one of five in New York City. The manpower shortage caused by the war had taken its toll on all sorts of occupations, and it had opened opportunities for otherwise unemployables. Although I was only twelve, with a work permit, I was able to get a job delivering newspapers.

I picked up the papers at a collection point after school, folded them, and stowed them in a carrier bag, which I fastened to my bicycle handlebars. Then off I went to deliver them, six days a week (no Sunday edition). Most of the subscribers lived in apartment buildings—four stories and no elevators. I didn't travel very far, but I did do a good deal of climbing up and down stairs. For my labors, I collected eighteen cents weekly from each subscriber. Economically, times were pretty good for civilians, and though I kept poor records, I was amazed at how many subscribers thought little of stiffing the newsboy of his hard-earned eighteen cents.

My carrier route was urbanized in small town fashion, with high density neighborhoods served by local merchants. People shopped on foot. Cars were scarce and gasoline rationed.

In the midst of my paper route was a Jewish delicatessen that sold kosher and other foods not found in the A&P supermarket where Mother did her grocery shopping. Tired, hungry, and with money in my pocket, I took to stopping into the delicatessen mid-route and experimenting with foods well beyond the pale of my normal diet. There was cheesecake, but it was not the cheesecake found here, which was contemptuously called cheese pie in Flushing. This cheesecake was made with cottage, not cream, cheese, and it came in immense rounds that sold by the pound. For eighteen cents, I got a substantial wedge offered on a piece of waxed butcher paper. It soon became a daily ritual.

In addition to cheesecake, they sold breads, both rounds and loaves in kinds I had never experienced. All shades of black, brown, yellow, and white. Some were laced or sprinkled with seeds, dried fruits, and even exotic, aromatic spices. They were all heavy and dense, with some weighing fourteen or fifteen pounds. Though less sweet than my favored cheesecake, I readily took a liking to these breads and from this derived a hearty contempt for Wonder bread.

Public schools with cafeterias in mid-century America provided a place indoors to sit and eat. Some offered milk or other beverages for sale, but none served lunches per se. Students brown-bagged their own lunches, which consisted routinely of sandwiches and perhaps a piece of fruit or candy. The sandwiches were invariably made with Wonder bread which had the advantage of being so soft it could be gummed or swallowed without chewing, no matter how bad your teeth were. Also, the bread never got stale, no matter how old it was, and it was cheap. This was no mean consideration in the days when typical families had four or more children to feed.

Knowing no better, a whole generation of American kids grew up thinking bread should taste and look like white sponge rubber; that it should be capable of being tube-fed. Undiluted; its crust should be crust in color only; and it should be useful principally as a clean, sanitary wrapper for otherwise messy foodstuffs, such as peanut butter and jelly, mashed potatoes with gravy, and baloney with mustard.

In the weekly cycle of domestic household chores, Monday was wash day, Friday was for housecleaning. In our family, Saturday was baking day. Whatever cakes, pies, and cookies were to be had in our house were made only on Saturdays. In our family, one did not purchase bakery products. By Tuesday, the week's supply exhausted, we kids were already anxiously awaiting Saturday. Mother was a competent cook, given her limited budget, and, having grown up on a farm, she was a good baker.

With my newly expanded delicatessen tastes, I asked her once why she never baked bread, as she readily admitted that, at her house, they had always done so. Wonder bread had not yet become widely available while she still lived at home. Didn't she like homemade bread? No way! To her, the homemade bread she was given as a child was that which her mother had found not fit to sell. She thought Wonder bread just fine.

For over half a century, I have been a heavy smoker—cigars, cigarettes, pipe. Whatever, if any, olfactory sense remains to me is severely impaired. Yet, of those aromas still detectable, I can think of none more pleasant, comforting, reassuring than that of bread baking. In the seventies, I had an office in Beverly Hills on Santa Monica Boulevard, not two blocks from a Wonder bread bakery. With the wind just right and the windows open, I marveled to realize that even such terrible stuff as Wonder bread could smell so good baking.

It is now many years since I discovered bread. In that time, I have sampled and delighted in fresh-baked rolls, baguettes, and croissants for breakfast in Paris, any number of substantial, chewy breadstuffs all over Europe, unleavened bread in Egypt, fantastic rounds in the Orient. Breads baked in ovens, fried over coals in a brazier, or fried in oil. It would surprise me if I had, during this time, eaten Wonder bread more than a dozen unavoidable times since leaving my parents' home.

Shortly after moving to Albuquerque in 1977, I discovered Indian bread, both the kind that is baked in an adobe *horno* and fry bread prepared in smoking oil. Fry bread must be eaten while hot and larded with honey or, even better, chile. It does not keep well. Oven bread can be sliced and frozen. Even after twenty years, toasted oven bread sets me salivating in such fashion as to make Pavlov proud.

Recently, we found a new source for a *Bauernbrot* in, of all places, Costco. This farmer's loaf has a crust to prove the merit of my plastic teeth, has body and flavor, and lists just four ingredients, of which water and sea salt are two. Like oatmeal, it stays with you.

Wealth is as you find it. It is for me sufficient I am not forced, for economy's sake, to eat Wonder bread.

Notes:

Wonder bread is used her as a generic term to describe an edible, sanitary packaging material for home use designed and promoted by the peanut butter-and-jelly industry to enhance the salability of their products, and which comes under a variety of trade names such as Rainbow, Helms, etc.

As balm to the guilty consciences of the mothers who foist this substance on their children, the bakers customarily list on the wrappers a whole host of vitamin additives to their bread, mute testimony to the otherwise nutritive poverty of their product.

An American tourist, traveling to Paris for the first time, stayed at a modest pension that included breakfast providing fresh rolls, brioche, baguettes, croissants with real butter, and preserves. The tourist was so taken with these breadstuffs that he inquired of the concierge where he got them. The concierge advised him that, each morning at six, he walked down the block to the bakery and bought fresh for their breakfasts. So impressed with the novelty and taste of the bread, the tourist asked if he could accompany the concierge and was promptly invited for the next morning.

Setting off afoot, the two walked in semidarkness no more than half a block before descending into the walk-down bakery. Inside, the air was so filled with fine flour dust that the tourist had difficulty seeing. He finally made out, in the dim light, the biggest, hairiest, man he'd ever seen, topless, sweating profusely, and wearing filthy, drooping pants, tearing off handfuls of dough and patting them into balls. When the ball of dough was shaped to his liking, the baker, for so he was, lifted his left arm, placed the ball in his sweaty, hairy armpit, and, bringing the left arm down smartly, squashed the ball into an oval, which the baker then tossed onto a large baking sheet preparatory to putting it, when full, into the oven.

"My god!" blurted out the tourist, "What is he doing?"

"Ah, monsieur," said the concierge, "but he is preparing the brioche of which you are so fond."

Almost retching, the tourist said, "That is the most disgusting thing I have ever seen!"

"Ah," replied the concierge, "but wait until you see him make bagels!"

Leslie

Susan to Sylvie, February 26, 2011

Dear Sylvie,

Attached is another of your grandfather's generic letters. Upon occasion, he asked me to proofread them. Sometimes he even relied on me to correct his spelling or syntax. I expressed surprise at the content of what follows, especially since the one I was proofreading would be sent to my mom, a bit of a prude at eighty.

Susan

Leslie's Letter, February 2000

Much of my adult life has been spent working with and for physicians on a business or personal, rather than consulting, basis for which I am forever grateful. Now, however, that I am fully retired and have reached the taxable age of mandatory withdrawal from my sheltered retirement funds, my medical contacts are more consistently professional. In a recent, rather thorough, physical examination by a new (to me) primary care physician, an endocrinologist by specialty, she commented, while digitally exploring my prostate, that my testicles were small.

My immediate reaction to the observation was that it was premature (if not impertinent) upon such brief examination, if her frame of reference was to my *cojones, mi machismo.* Challenged, she explained that her observation was strictly anatomical; her concern was with testosterone output, whose level she would order tested, along with that of a battery of other hormones.

Driving home afterward, my thoughts took to task her observation. I speculated that now was a hell of a time to discover I was testosterone-deficient. I was unaware that my sex life, in which, admittedly, fact often lagged behind fancy, might have been distorted by a hormonal deficiency. Despite Bob Dole's recent advocacy of performance enhancing medications, I felt no unreasonable spread between performance and expectation. Then the thought occurred to me that, like the aged alcoholic, finally forced to admit to his alcoholism, exclaimed, "and all this time I merely thought I was Irish!" Perhaps my experience in this matter lay, like my cholesterol level, outside the limits of normal.

My mind would not let go. My God! What if I had been advised I was testicularly challenged at the age of thirteen, fourteen, fifteen? My future would have crumbled. Knowledge of so sensitive a nature could in no way be kept secret. How could I ever face gym? The showers? The humiliation? What girl would have been seen even talking to me, never mind dating me?

I could picture the "jocks" talking at our twenty-fifth high school reunion. "Freeman? Leslie Freeman? No, I don't think… oh, wait, you mean 'little balls.' Yeah, I remember him! Remember the time we…" My more sexually active years would have been plagued with the thought I might be underperforming.

Stop it! So? So what? We pass this way but once!

A follow-up visit is scheduled, at which the endocrinologist will read the tarot cards of my hormonal test profile. In equanimity, I can wait.

Leslie

Susan to Sylvie, February 28, 2011

Dear Sylvie,

My box of treasures, the one you will someday receive, is cloth covered, no larger than an average man's shoe box. It contains a handkerchief Leslie gave me in 1975 to wipe away my tears, a few cards, an inscribed paper bag, and our letters to one another. Prized among them is. the attached, commemorating our fourteenth wedding anniversary.

Susan

Leslie to Susan, April 25, 1998

Dear Susan,

Do we count our blessings? Not often enough. Shortcomings, too often.

Fourteen years (out of twenty-five [?]) are we now married. An unorthodox courtship, a storybook wedding, a first for neither of us and, if wiser, therefore entered into with no less trepidation.

Marrying a woman twenty years younger (is it time yet to start shaving off a few years?) after seven years of bachelorhood, taking her halfway around the world in ways measured in more than miles, into an environment as different from Southern California and North Dakota as it could be, away from family and friends and with a man she hasn't seen in over three years!

Cocky? Foolhardy? Or, in hindsight, just plain prescient.

Whatever reservations I may have nursed on that long flight from Jeddah faded with my first sight of you waiting for me there, at the base of the escalator in LAX, fourteen years ago. Memory betrayed me. You were even more beautiful than I remembered. Your behavior during our brief honeymoon and even more so in those first few months with so much new and alien proved your beauty, once again, as much, much more than skin deep.

Again, with the benefit of hindsight, it should have been no surprise that the euphoria of life in the Middle Eastern cocoon of AMI carried us through those first years back in the real life of Albuquerque. Those premarital trepidations, fears, and hopes have now been subjected to the reality of fourteen years and proven as wide of the mark as most are—and as likely to be as far off again as today's will be fourteen years from now. If expectations have narrowed, some things have grown in value.

Wrinkles aside, I am still married to the most beautiful woman I know. A woman with a wondrous sense of humor and a disposition to match, an essential lubricant to the frictions of life with LFF.

I loved you twenty-five years ago, fourteen years ago, yesterday, and will go on loving you for the rest of my life, or the next fourteen, whichever comes first.

Leslie loves Susan.

Susan to Sylvie, March 2, 2011

Dear Sylvie,

After attaching Leslie's anniversary letter, I realized you probably don't know where we spent our honeymoon. Your romantic grandfather planned that we would wed in Gibraltar and honeymoon on the waters of the Mediterranean. Because of a visa glitch, the specifics long since forgotten, we wed in La Crescenta, California, and honeymooned near the waters of the Pacific Ocean. As we arrived at the church, we realized that the license was left in our hotel room. We explained to Reverend O'Connor our oversight, and he said it was not a problem. He was visiting a relative close to the hotel and would drop by to sign immediately after the ceremony. Leslie dropped me off to retrieve the license, and he proceeded to park the rental car. When I returned to the hotel lobby where we had agreed to meet, I first saw Leslie drive round and round trying to find a parking place, followed by the good reverend. When we eventually gathered round the lobby table, Reverend O'Connor got on his knees, pen in hand, ready to make us officially wed, explaining that he had cataracts. The hotel clerk happily provided her autograph as witness. No one ever believed that we enjoyed ham hocks and lima beans at Marie Callender's for our wedding dinner.

Our honeymoon commenced at Cambria Pines Lodge, located between the famous landmarks of Hearst Castle and Morro Bay, with peacocks parading the spacious grounds, announcing their procession with a screaming meow. We had called ahead and were told that only one room was available the first night, in an old cabin slated for demolition the following week. It had one twin bed (you might not want to know, but it was large enough for romantic endeavors) and ivy growing through a crack in the wall. For recompense, they presented us with a bottle of champagne and a blackberry cobbler to celebrate our marriage.

In sorting through our letters, I discovered the first of what were to become my journal entries in Al Baha, although this one was written five days after we married. Your grandfather took a daily nap; it didn't have to be long, but nap he did, and thus I would have had time to write the following.

<u>April 30, 1984—St. Helena, California, Heart of the Wine Country</u>

Our life together surpasses my greatest expectations. What I had felt for Leslie in the past was only rudimentary, and I thought it overwhelming then. The one great love a person dreams of, we share. I never knew I could be so happy. I wondered if I could ever love a man completely. I can and do. Whatever he does, he devotes himself to fully, be it is interest in local artifacts or a conversation, and I revel in the times when the devotion is mine and mine alone. He is a private man, and that part of himself which has been closed to others is open to me. I know I had to be the person I am now before I committed myself to him. My darling Leslie, I can even say those words to him.

Susan

August 2000, a year before we knew that Leslie had cancer

Stage IV

Susan to Sylvie, March 6, 2011

Dear Sylvie,

The past weeks have been a mental journey through the most enjoyable years of my life. Now I begin trudging through the most difficult, a journey with unfamiliar signposts, ones reading "wrong way," "exit only," and, finally, "dead end."

Leslie's leaving me began in the summer of 2000. He had built a portico in the patio and was painting the beams when his right shoulder began to ache. He attributed it to unused muscles. By year-end, the pain was sufficient to induce him to seek medical advice. A battery of tests, X-rays, CT scan, and blood work proved nothing conclusive. Since he was seventy years of age, it was probable he had arthritis. Therapy and a regimen of stretching exercises were recommended and provided a brief respite from the pain.

Your grandfather's lifelong love of tennis began when he was eleven. Only a vacation or the promise of an adventure-filled weekend would prevent him from Sunday tennis. Southern California and Albuquerque provided ideal year-round playing conditions. When he gave up tennis, I feared that it was more than arthritis.

As a teenager, Leslie was an avid soccer player but was asked to leave the team after repeated smoking violations. Saturday mornings at Boston University were spent smoking cigars and listening to the Met—another of his lifelong loves, opera. When cigarettes reached thirty-five cents a pack, he switched to pipes. A friend expressed surprise that he inhaled pipe tobacco. His response, "Why smoke, if you don't inhale?"

August 15, 2001, was the beginning of our last journey together. Under general anesthesia, a biopsy was performed of his lymph nodes, and surrounding tissue was excised from his right armpit. For what seemed hours, I further smoothed the industrial vinyl of a hospital corridor until the surgeon approached me. He shook my hand and said, "I'm sorry."

"I'm sorry." The biopsy results confirmed the surgeon's visual observation of Stage IV, inoperable, metastatic cancer, Pancoast Syndrome, a lung cancer presenting in 12 percent of cases. The malignant tumor hid on the apex of Leslie's right lung. It had not invaded the lung but had branched out into his right arm and spread to other parts of his body.

We read everything we could find about Pancoast Syndrome and treatment modalities. And we learned that few survive Stage IV lung cancer. The oncologist recommended an immediate course of radiation to reduce the tumor. This would only be a palliative measure. After Leslie's extensive readings regarding chemo and potential side effects, he decided that the extra six to twelve months of life were not worth the price. Based on Pancoast histories, the cancer would metastasize to the liver, kidneys, adrenal glands, and/or to the brain.

Your grandfather continued his monthly letter writing and shared with us his last odyssey, leaving a blueprint on how to face death with humor and dignity.

Susan

Leslie's Letter, August 29, 2001

Sparked, perhaps, by wishful thinking, rumor has it my demise is imminent, which is surely an exaggeration although, as a still all-too-prominent public figure might claim, it is strictly a matter of how imminent is imminent, since demise we must all.

To set the matter straight, there is good news, and there is news.

The good news is the discomfort that has been bugging my right shoulder and arm is not tendonitis nor arthritis. It is lung cancer. To be more specific, metastasis adenocarcinoma Stage IV non-small-cell lung carcinoma, Pancoast Syndrome. With this definitive a description, any hopes that this case might be sufficiently unique as to merit a new chapter in the medical annals are dashed, and I probably won't even earn a footnote in some obscure statistical table.

After more than fifty years of amateur tennis and serious smoking, I must now give up tennis. Which serves to prove my avowed advice never to voluntarily give up any vices, for surely they will be taken away from you soon enough. There is some comfort to be taken in that we have been reassured this is not a sexually transmissible disease.

The medical oncologist Susan and I interviewed recommended that six weeks of radiation, five days per week, be completed and assessed before even thinking about chemotherapy. Asked about longevity, his evasions notwithstanding, he finally admitted that, with a bit of luck, maybe a year. Since the radiation oncology group providing the treatments is under contract to the HMO providing my care, I figure they will be on my side, and that, realistically, gives me a window of six weeks to twelve months, just about enough time to balance last month's bank statement.

My chest looks like a road map broadly inked in with a magic marker; it even has a tattooed X to mark the spot at which to aim the radiological magic bullets.

It has been a long time since I thought the ideal way to end this sojourn would be without warning, to simply not wake up one morning. Not so. Too messy, too traumatic for the survivors. Easy enough for the one who dies. You need do nothing; it is all done to and for you. It is the caregivers who do all the suffering and then have to wash the dishes and put them away when it is over. Not fair. Much nicer to have a bit of notice, a bit of time to tidy things up, to share with those closest to you this final, greatest experience of life.

We all came into this world alone, and that is how we will leave. But, since the fact is that I had little enough to say about how I came in, it is comforting to think I may have something to do about how I exit.

All of this, mind you, while, with the exception of the pain in my shoulder, I remain symptom-free. No weight loss (unfortunately), good appetite, sleep well, no shortness of breath, unreconstructed sense of humor. However, should the weather change…

Many thanks to all of you who have shown such considerate restraint and not phoned this past month. E-mail is fine, nondisruptive; sometimes we even read it. We'll try to keep you posted.

Leslie

Sylvie to Susan, March 11, 2011

Dear Susan,

How sad I was when Grandpa died. Although I think Mom acts pretty stoic about his death, I know that she misses him. I can't imagine how it must be for you without him, after reading your letters and now knowing how much you loved him.

When we visited before Grandpa died, I remember one night he was sitting in his chair and you went over and knelt beside him and placed your head in his lap, not saying a word, oblivious to us.

You wrote that I could ask you questions as I read your letters. You haven't shared what it was like for you, as Grandpa said, as the caregiver who suffers.

Sylvie

Susan to Sylvie, March 16, 2011

Dear Sylvie,

I've tried to keep the focus on what your grandfather felt and wrote; I've never explained what I felt that awful day when I heard, "I'm sorry." After the surgeon left, I sought refuge in an empty waiting room and called our friend Diane to tell her the results. When I hung up, I cried. After composing myself, I went to the recovery room and sat by Leslie, waiting for him to return to a world no longer the same. The nurses were talking and laughing, and I wanted to scream at them, *shut up, shut up, how can you be so insensitive when my husband has been handed a death sentence, how can you laugh when all I want to do is cry*. But I didn't scream. And I didn't cry. I stroked his arm and watched his beloved face, and I made a silent vow. I would honor whatever he chose to do.

After he was released from the hospital, I drove home, talking aimlessly, hoping he wouldn't ask the results. But he did, and I told him, "Let's get home, I'll fix you lunch, and then we'll talk." He ate his lunch on the patio, a splendid summer's day, the kind he loved so much, and then I told him. He didn't change his expression. He just puffed on his pipe as I answered his questions.

Your grandfather was a dignified man. He treated his impending death as he did any other element of his life: with reflection, calmness, and a measure of levity. I realize that his dignity helped me to be strong. I was no longer the emotional coward. It didn't stop me from crying, though. Most days I would go to my bathroom, shut the door, and cry into a towel.

Susan

Sylvie to Susan, March 21, 2011

Dear Susan,

Thank you for sharing your feelings and memories. I loved Grandpa; he was the first person I cared for who died. I think Grandpa Leslie was a Catholic, but Mom never mentioned attending a Catholic church: she's an atheist.

Sylvie

Susan to Sylvie, March 26, 2011

Dear Sylvie,

Leslie was raised a Roman Catholic, but when he was a young adult, the capital C became lower-case. We spent a lot of time in places of worship during our years together, from the grandeur of Paris's Notre Dame and Istanbul's Blue Mosque to our own New Mexico mud and straw churches. We even attended Mass one Christmas Eve in Hernandez, New Mexico. If pressed, I would state my belief in God, but I didn't believe in life after death. Leslie would answer simply that he was agnostic. Leslie was aware of your mom's beliefs. He wrote her that it took more backbone than he could claim to actually commit to disbelief.

The attached explains his religious feelings, rather than beliefs. I am also attaching some of the letters and updates Leslie sent the last months of his life.

Susan

Leslie's Letter, October 26, 2001

Upon entering Belmont High School, I tested my devotion to the religious life by completing three years of Latin under the tutelage of a classic example of an aging spinster, who astounded me in my final year when she was revealed to be a gifted comedienne, when we both performed in the senior/

faculty play, *A Yankee in King Arthur's Court*. At my father's insistence, I entered Boston University rather than the seminary I would have preferred.

In my freshman year, a course in comparative religion revealed to me the similarities in moral precepts between almost all civilized major religions and the multitude of dogmas differentiating them—and in whose name the propagation thereof perpetrated the most calamitous slaughters history has known. End of my calling.

While living at home, I continued to attend to the obligatory duties of a practicing Roman Catholic in order to forestall conflict within the family, but once on my own, I abandoned the charade. I became an agnostic, believing in and denying none. I find difficulty in accepting another's revealed truth, claim none of my own, and, if I did, would hesitate to proselytize, as I resent other's attempts to do so to me. Yet, I don't claim to be amoral. I simply don't feel a commission to evangelize my beliefs.

This said, I have spent many happy hours in churches of all kinds. Some have excellent acoustics, and there is much of sacred music that is enhanced by performance within such edifices, with or without associated pageantry. In addition, civilization's architectural heritage is greatly dependent upon those buildings devoted to religious purposes.

Only twice have I actually made a religious retreat. First, in my high school years, to a Trappist Monastery in Connecticut, which may qualify as a religious experience, and then most recently to the Christ in the Desert Monastery in New Mexico, which would not qualify.

My agnosticism doesn't preclude mystical experience, of which I can recount innumerable events, some of them within a religious environment such as the Christ in the Desert Monastery. The beauty of the sound of Gregorian chants, sung *a cappella* in plainsong, heard in the semidarkness of a chapel in remote Northern New Mexico, as the dawn sun gradually illuminates the interior, a night spent on a beach at the shore of the Red Sea with the stars, unimpeded by the light of civilization, for a blanket and with the gentle wash of surf lulling one to sleep is conducive for me to such experiences. A notable rendition of an aria from one of my favorite operas, a wild sunset in remoteness, the artistry of a fine craftsman (stone mason, wood carver) in architectural detail—any of these can provide a moment immeasurable out of the ordinary consciousness into the realm of mysticism. These moments have sufficed to fill any void I may have felt in the absence of those comforts others have found in religious faith.

In response to our last letter, we have enjoyed a steady procession of considerately scheduled visits of family members and friends, with more yet to come—to say nothing of notes and e-mail messages offering assistance in abundance.

A few surprises. Those of you who have come to visit have all remarked on how well I look, casting the shadow of doubt upon the gravity of the situation. I shall probably have to cultivate a more hangdog appearance, affect a limp, or adopt a more plaintive speech pattern to sustain your preconceived image and sympathy. Ah, the burdens of a graceful demise. The restraint from all in offering, but not stressing, spiritual counseling. I do have reservations about the process of dying but, unlike Hamlet, no fear of death itself. So be it.

Six weeks of radiation therapy are now behind me. The treasure map of markers on my shoulder has been bleached out, a bit of residual radiation burn yet to go, but no more pain in the shoulder and arm! No more need for ibuprofen. At my exit interview with the radiation oncologist, I expressed my concern with atrophy of the muscles in my right arm from disuse and asked whether it was advisable for me to consider attempting to play tennis again or would I be risking further damage to weakened tissues (bone and muscle). His answer? "That's a good question!" Equivocation! Last Sunday, I tried a set of tennis.

No immediate or to date ill effect. Remission, temporary or otherwise, thy name is happiness.

In the flush of well-being, following the completion of radiation therapy, I find no difficulty in sustaining my conceit that the end of my mortal life is only natural, not a sentence, and that I shall face it in peace, without the comfort of a religious conviction.

Leslie

Susan to Sylvie, March 28, 2011

Dear Sylvie,

Among the many letters, cards and e-mail messages we were receiving daily, a friend asked Leslie to share his insights on life. He wrote to Leslie, "From our first acquaintance, you impressed me with your self-assurance, intrepid nature, and independent spirit. You are one of the few people I have known who have climbed out of the expected rut their life was to be, and not just traveled, but lived in other worlds. I have learned that strange food, squat toilets, intestinal parasites, and bedbugs are not quite as exotic as the travel brochure, but that doesn't take anything away from the person who accepts difficulties as part of the entrance fee to life."

Attached is Leslie's response to his younger friend's inquiry.

Susan

Leslie's Letter, December 1, 2001

There are still many societies today where the wisdom and advice of the elders is respected. This is not one of the many virtues of our American society. While we still continue in our belief that wisdom comes from age and experience, it is a great disappointment to discover in one's old age that there is a very small market for such, especially from one's own children. It is, therefore, flattering to have it sought. Thank you.

Put in this position and invited to express myself along these lines, it is embarrassing to discover that the pearls of wisdom personally discovered seem so trite! That many of those we can now personally attest have already been handed down through the generations (and so causally perused in our youth) really makes sense. How humbling.

When subjected to the test of experience, some of these gems are discovered to apply only with many qualifications. Different interpretations of "anything worth doing is worth doing well" can make an excellent excuse for doing nothing and raises the question, does it apply to robbing banks? And "experience is the best teacher" does that qualify Mickey Rooney as an authority on marriage, or one need acquire AIDS in order to prove to oneself that unprotected sex can be hazardous?

My intent is not to be facetious but to point out that there are hazards in offering advice, due to overly literal interpretation carried to extremes and misinterpretation of meaning.

So, having qualified my advice, let me confine myself to three of my personal jewels. Lighten up! The real world is best seen in shades of gray! To thine own self be true!

If laughter is not the best medicine, it is pretty close, much cheaper when the subject is yourself, and the most effective. The stronger your conviction, the more in need it is of humor—as opposed to levity—from you, not others.

Black, white, and color are merely accents and may confuse our real vision of people, events, and the world around us. Experience can enhance our individual perspective, from which we are able to broaden our ability to distinguish the infinite variation in shades of gray.

I've known what's right from wrong since I was ten. Almost all of the things I regret have been done in violation of what I've known was right. What I've known to be right and wrong didn't always conform to the letter of the law from Moses or the Constitution. This doesn't relieve me of the responsibility of being subject to those jurisdictions. Render unto Jesus and to Caesar. The ultimate judgment is the knowledge of what is right and wrong.

Enough wisdom.

For many men, there comes a time in their forties or fifties when they suddenly can see clearly the road ahead. A revelation! For some, a shock. No, no, no! This is not the course I set out upon, how did I not see it coming? Your options have slowly closed in on you. What to do? Midlife crisis! Welcome to the club.

First thing to do is panic. Indulge it for a while, you'll get over it. In small doses, self-pity is therapeutic. Second, lighten up. Then, start thinking about where you want to be. Don't be afraid to confess to and consult with those closest to you; they have a vested interest—that was my biggest mistake.

You are at the height of your powers, even if, in your current dissatisfaction, you don't feel that way. Evaluate your assets and liabilities, and go from there. More specific I cannot be.

I look upon the years from forty-five to sixty-five as the best in my life. I do not regret the first forty-five, for the experience of them made me pretty much what I became and was at age forty-five. They gave me the courage to set out on open and uncharted waters.

Leslie

Susan to Sylvie, March 30, 2011

Dear Sylvie,

Thanksgiving and Christmas 2001 were bittersweet, as we knew that they would be our last ones together. It was a time of year Leslie thoroughly enjoyed, for he had two turkey dinners within a month. Sometimes we would go to one of the pueblos on Christmas Eve to observe a traditional Indian Pueblo midnight mass, complete with native dances. This year, it was enough to be together, to be at home with family and friends.

As customary, Leslie wrote his thank-you after-Christmas letter, which I have attached, summarizing the gifts we received. There was the usual pilfered *New Yorker* cartoon. A physician sits at his desk telling his middle-aged male patient, "It appears that you'll definitely outlive your usefulness."

Susan

Leslie's Letter, January 4, 2002

Already the days grow longer, and, oh my, do we need the month of January. Aptly named by the Romans for their two-faced god, Janus, patron of beginnings and endings, but after the excesses of the year ending, we need those thirty-one days of respite to face the beginning of a new year. Not that the ending was all that excessive for us, but there was news enough during the year that, even in the absence of a clean slate, we are quite ready for a new start.

None of which detracted from our pleasure in celebrating the holidays almost continuously for ten days. Nothing riotous, you understand, since at my age, four ounces of dry sherry is as close to whoopee as I get, and when ten o'clock rolls round, bedtime is well-nigh irresistible.

Thinking of sherry, ever notice the warning on the prescription label, *do not take with alcohol?* Well, if you read the small print on the container insert listing the side effects that may be encountered with use, it notes that ingesting it with alcohol may enhance these effects. Since drowsiness and mild euphoria are often listed, try it. Now, I never take my ibuprofen or morphine without. Works just fine.

Pretty good year for presents, not a bummer in the group, plenty of books and the biggest surprise of all, in the International Star Registry, star number Aquarius RA 23h 12m 23s D-17'7" will henceforth be known as the Leslie F. Freeman star, as duly attested in a framed certificate to this effect now hanging in our garage, just behind the water heater. Along with the certificate came a framed map of that portion of the celestial sky showing the coordinates of the Aquarius constellation in which the Leslie F. Freeman star (fifth magnitude) is circled in red. For those of you unfamiliar with celestial observation, a fifth magnitude star is one of such brightness that on a clear night, it is readily visible to the naked eye of one with eyesight of 1,000/20 or with a sixteen-inch reflecting telescope.

Unfortunately, when Aquarius is up, I am not. Lacking the necessary visual acuity or sixteen-inch telescope, it is doubtful I will get to see my namesake in the immediate future. But, with all of this official documentation, one could hardly doubt the existence of such an honor. Henceforth, you may refer to me as Leslie F. Freeman, FCO (Fellow of the Celestial Order). It won't be necessary for you to bow when we meet, you may just kiss my Flash Gordon ring with secret compartment.

The history of civilization is replete with the essential role that martyrs and saints have played in its evolution, but for my reading of them, I would not have wanted to be married to one. For the most part, they were rather unpleasant people: confrontational, intolerant of dissenting opinions, they sanctified or condemned, depending upon whether you agreed or disagreed with their causes. Mother Teresa notwithstanding, they also tended to have rather short lives and most unpleasant demises.

Not for me. I'm a middle-of-the-roader. Let the extremists extend equidistant to the left and right of my course in life. If some have viewed my conduct as otherwise, meriting either beatification or condemnation, save me please from such opinions. Post-mortem, there will be time enough. Only remember, *de mortuis, nil nisi bonum.*

Leslie

Susan to Sylvie, April 1, 2011

Dear Sylvie,

By mid-January a growth was visible on Leslie's right cheek, twisting his facial muscles into a fixed, crooked grin. The pain medication was increased. Only once did I see him display any visible emotion for the physical changes and pain he was experiencing. It was the evening he told me that the latest CT scan revealed that the cancer had spread to the adrenal glands. It was momentary and ever so slight.

His cartoon for the attached letter depicted a man sitting under a hospital admissions sign. The admitting clerk was handing him a stringed form, advising him to "Fill out this tag and attach it to your big toe."

Susan

Leslie's Letter, January 26, 2002

Dear Siblings,

The news you have all been waiting for—medical update (lightly varnished).

Metastatic intrusion of the cancer has now been established by CT scan into the adrenal gland and muscle mass of the left hip, confirmed by needle biopsy. Most recently, involvement of the parietal (salivary) gland in my right cheek has also been confirmed. The medical oncologist has recommended chemotherapy; the radiation oncologist, focal treatment of the two areas. Either treatment modality would be palliative, not curative.

At the moment, I am more inclined to the radiation approach, since chemotherapy statistically offers only a 35 percent success rate, defined as an increase of six months in longevity, with a list of possible side effects which, if compared to those of anticipated symptoms from no treatment at all, do not differ greatly. Six more months of pharmacological treatment of symptoms from either natural or treatment causes has little appeal. Regardless of duration, my recent experience with radiation therapy has been relatively painless and has provided total remission from discomfort in my shoulder. Just started a series of fourteen radiation treatments on my right cheek, hoping for success.

In the meantime, although I lack for energy and sleep an average of ten hours per day, my weight and appetite stay constant, and my discomfort level is sustained within tolerable levels by a diet of painkillers with minimal side effects. Incidentally, while on this subject, should any of you suffer a bout of diarrhea, I have discovered a most effective remedy.

The crooked grin my face exhibits is not due to any change in my sense of humor; it is merely the effect of attempting to smile with the loss of muscle control on the right side of my face. Vanity inclines me to adopt a mask or veil, perhaps even a *burqa*. I understand that, on the used clothing market, they will soon be in glut in Afghanistan.

Until our shipment of *burqas* arrive, Susan and I regret that we will not be able to entertain visitors. We ask your understanding.

Will try to keep you posted.

Leslie

Susan to Sylvie, April 3, 2011

Dear Sylvie,

When we first returned to Albuquerque, Leslie took me exploring to the many places he enjoyed in our Land of Enchantment. Together we witnessed my first Native American dance at Jemez Pueblo, a *matachine*, his favorite. We camped in a snow storm in Chaco Canyon, crossed the Plains of San Agustin that reminded us of the Mongolian grasslands, and discovered our favorite place to camp and hike, Ghost Ranch.

The many explorations of northern New Mexico began with Leslie's employment as controller of a plant located in our own Las Vegas. Leslie writes of an experience in 1986, a letter which I have attached. The accompanying cartoon presented a husband telling his wife, "You can wrap it up in a pretty package, but it's still life."

Susan

Leslie's Letter, February 2002

Even before the transcontinental railroad came through in the early 1880s, Las Vegas, New Mexico, was an important trading center on the old Santa Fe trail, due to its proximity to Fort Union, the major military supply and ordinance depot for much of Texas and the territories of what became New Mexico and Arizona. The building of the railroad added significantly to an already bustling economy, supplying goods and services to the fort and commercial traffic on the trail. By the time statehood came to New Mexico in 1912, Las Vegas was already a political powerhouse in the capital of Santa Fe.

Located on the southeastern edge of the southernmost tip of the Rocky Mountains, the Great Plains extend eastward clear to the Missouri River, in rolling grasslands that used to feed huge herds of buffalo supporting roving bands of Native American tribes. The buffalo are now mostly gone, replaced by cattle and ranchers, and the Indian tribes are restricted to reservations.

When I was offered a job in Las Vegas, I accepted readily, even though it meant taking an apartment, living there during the work week, and commuting two hours home to Susan on weekends.

Our initial affection for the people and countryside around Las Vegas grew with time, to the extent that Susan would come up on occasional weekends to enjoy and explore, once even taking the train from Albuquerque to Las Vegas.

On one of those weekends, we attended a working cowboy rodeo held at the county fairgrounds out on the edge of town. Now, a working cowboy rodeo does share some events with the professional rodeos, such as calf roping and occasionally bronc and bull riding, but it doesn't attract the professionals. It is basically a hometown event, an opportunity for the local cowboys to demonstrate their prowess in everyday working skills, handling their mounts, and in cutting and herding stock. On that day's schedule, we were reasonably familiar with most of the events, but the one that attracted our attention was milking a range cow.

The open-air arena was ovoid in shape, with the long axis east to west. Along the southern fence were shaded bleachers with the judge's boxes strung along the northern side. To the east were the stock holding pens; a large, double-hung mesh fence gate on the west faced out onto the open range beyond.

The day was beautiful, the scenery spectacular, the spectators sparse. Not more than a couple of dozen of us were in the bleachers, most of whom, from their overheard conversation, seemed to be related to the participants or organizers of the rodeo. We watched a few events with no more than five or six entrants, in which contestants performed with good humor, competence, but little flash. And then came time for the range cow milking.

Never having even heard of, much less watched, such an event, it was explained to us that the object of this contest was to collect, in a small wide-mouthed bottle, visible evidence of cow's milk to the judges. The first to do so was declared winner. The contestants were teams, one mounted to rope the cow, the other afoot to milk and present the evidence.

Three teams lined up at the west end of the arena, just in front of the closed gate. Three cows, two considerably larger than the third, were prodded out the chute into the arena at the east end, facing the milkers. Range cows, who have given birth and nursed out on the open range, with little, if any, exposure to humans, are pretty independent, aggressive in defense of their prerogatives as mothers, and easily spooked.

After milling nervously at their end of the arena, the three impressively horned cows arranged themselves facing the riders and, lowering their heads, pawed the ground in front of them. More like something one might expect at Pamplona. They didn't look like cows to the uneducated me.

At a signal from the judges, the three riders took off for the cows, lariats at the twirl, the grounded cowboys following. Now a mounted cowboy can be a thrilling combination of horse and man in graceful coordination. A cowboy running afoot, encumbered by boots designed for riding ease and holding a small glass bottle in his outstretched hand, is not.

The three wary cows, eyeing the approach of the cowboys and thinking, perhaps, that this was something akin to a medieval joust, took out at a full run directly for the cowboys and, with ease, broke through their ranks, and, not pausing, burst through the closed gate, slamming one side of it against the parked standby ambulance just outside, leaving its convex flank with a huge converse dent. At which point we heard the woman sitting next to us exclaim, "Oh my God, we didn't get insurance! There goes our profits," as we watched the three cows disappearing into the open range beyond.

Nonplussed, the judges ordered three more cows brought into the arena, the contestants returned to the starting line, and the judges signaled for a new beginning.

As before, the cowboys raced out, but these cows performed differently. One spooked, jumped over the chute gate, and trotted off, back to the holding pen. The other two scattered, hotly pursued by all three riders, one of whom, after several unsuccessful attempts, got his rope firmly around the horns of one of the cows.

Even when the other end of the animal is firmly attached to a rope held by your mounted partner, approaching an angry, eleven-hundred-pound wild cow from the rear, on foot, armed only with a small glass bottle, and with intent to milk the cow, strikes me as an unequal contest.

The trick, as we learned later, is for the milker to get his hand firmly onto a teat, at which point, the mother cow immediately calm down, believing that the milker's hand is her calf's mouth. This calls for a measure of faith in animal instinct quite beyond my level of confidence. As amazed as we were amused, we watched the cowboy extract enough fluid to then run to the judges with proof of his team's win, while the remaining cow tore around the arena, still pursued by the two less-fortunate teams.

This may not rank up there with some of the gladiatorial spectacles staged by the ancient Romans, but in Las Vegas, New Mexico, could one ask more of entertainment for a weekend?

Leslie

Susan to Sylvie, April 7, 2011

Dear Sylvie,

February is Freeman birthday month—not only your grandfather, but your mom and aunt celebrate another life's year. By late February the facial radiation therapy was complete and had successfully reduced the swelling and discomfort in Leslie's cheek. Per his request, only your family, your Aunt Amy's family, and a few close friends in Albuquerque visited.

He spent the days arranging pictures from our time in Arabia and our memorable trips, sorting through his writings over the years, and disposing of clothes and art supplies, and even parting with his treasured tennis rackets. At night, he maintained his habit of reading for two or three hours.

Attached is his family medical update, affixed with a cartoon of an older couple strolling through town. He quips, "For some reason, I'm getting nicer. Where will it end?"

Susan

Leslie's Letter, March 4, 2002

Medical update:

Item: The course of radiation on my right cheek has now been completed. The swelling over the parietal gland has been reduced, the discomfort eliminated, and there is nothing left to show for it but a skin burn that looks very much like a strawberry birthmark; they have assured me it will soon clear up.

Item: Today I start a series of fourteen daily similar treatments to my left hip in anticipation of a comparable outcome. Having been successful with the two previous series of radiation treatments to diminish the pain, I look forward to the completion of this last treatment series, knowing the effect is purely palliative and of relatively short duration.

Otherwise, my weight remains stable, appetite normal, with the congestion in the lower end of my gastrointestinal tract manageable with an occasional dose of milk of magnesium and softener. The only noticeable effect is continuing lack of energy.

There is compensation, however, in the diminishing level of responsibility for my future and the offers of support, help, and expressions of sympathy from friends and family, which often come in unexpected ways. Those who would normally not hesitate to interrupt my discourse now listen to my opinions (regardless of how ill-founded) as oracular pronouncements. Susan no longer tells me, "You're not going to wear that tie with that shirt, are you?" My children don't tell me, "You need Scope!"

My greatest concern is how best to take advantage of the situation and, of course, how to extend it. Then there is that little matter of how to handle the waiter when he finally brings the check. I'm working on it.

Leslie

Susan to Sylvie, April 10, 2011

Dear Sylvie,

April used to be my favorite month—my birth month and our anniversary. In preparing to send you Leslie's last monthly letter, it struck me that his written reflections keep going back in time. The previous letter, which I did not share with you, recounted an Army experience that occurred around 1954. The attached goes back to 1945.

His last letter is a testament to his unique character. I think most of us, at least I would, use it as a forum for a final farewell.

Susan

Leslie's Letter, April 2002

In the fall of 1951, having completed undergraduate work and spent the summer pot walloping in the coastal resort town of Ogunquit, Maine, I set out in a new 1951 Plymouth station wagon, with a friend, to drive from Cambridge to Berkeley in order to deliver the car to a professor who had recently transferred and was pleased to trade transport for us to deliver his vehicle. Never having traveled west of the Hudson River, and with two weeks for the run, it was quite an attractive offer. My companion, a recent grad from Harvard, was returning home to Dallas; I was heading to Southern California to rejoin my family, who had moved there the previous year.

Needless to say, it was quite an adventure. New exposures of all kinds at a time when I was ripe for them, but for many years, the expanse from the Rocky Mountains to the Sierra Nevadas was a complete wasteland of uninteresting desert in my memory. Gradually, over a period of twenty years in California, the nuances and beauty of the topography, color, plant and animal life, and history (ancient and modern) of this vast region began to obsess me. It does today. The real opportunity to pursue this interest didn't occur until I moved to Albuquerque in 1977. It hasn't stopped.

Thirty miles north of Portland, Maine, lies Crystal Lake, upon whose shores the Catholic Diocese of Portland maintained a summer camp for children. How I ended up there in the summer of 1945 is lost to memory, but there I was, kitchen help to the cooks. The camp nurse was an imposing, middle-aged woman, meticulous in her housekeeping, kept reasonably busy ministering to the children's various colds, rashes, cuts, and bruises, with usually one or two of them in residence at the dispensary. Short of temper and caustic of tongue, she was not particularly well-liked. But she commanded all of our respect for her medical competence, and, from those few of us who smoked, our undying allegiance, for as a heavy smoker herself, she tolerated those who indulged upon the broad porch of her dispensary after hours.

After supper, one long summer evening, a select few were indulging upon the porch, trading gossip of the day, when a small group approached, carrying a camper who had cut himself on broken glass. The camper's foot was bleeding generously. The nurse intercepted the new arrivals and admonished them not to bring the injured into the dispensary to bleed all over her clean floor. She advised them to set him down on the porch steps and disappeared inside, reemerging with a tray of medical supplies, including bandages, surgical tape, cotton balls, and ether, with which she was accustomed to cleaning such wounds.

Having cleaned the wound, discarded the ether-soaked cotton balls into a handy wastebasket, and dressed the wound, the nurse discharged the patient with an appropriate admonition to be more careful in the future. The camper gone, she took her tools of trade back inside and rejoined us on the porch, lighting up as she sat down. Perhaps distracted by the interruption, she carelessly discarded her match into the wastebasket, which immediately erupted with a spectacular *whoosh*. It took at least a week before she had regained her composure, at which time we were once again allowed to join her on the dispensary porch of an evening.

It was also at Camp Gregory that I had my first taste of beer. The occasion was VJ Day. One of the staff had slipped out of camp and returned with a case of beer in quarts; smaller containers were not yet popular. Lacking cups but not initiative, we raided the camp chapel and borrowed a number of red glass votive-candle holders, some still with a waxy rind, with which to share the bounty. Unwilling to acknowledge my uninitiated status, I accepted a cup full and manfully drained half of it with the first draught.

Piss! They have tricked me with a cup full of piss! I looked carefully about my fellow imbibers, seeking evidence of who among them was in on the joke, but all seemed much too enthused over the celebration to be paying any attention to my discomfort. Only partially reassured that I was mistaken, I still couldn't finish my drink. It was months before I was willing to try a drink of beer again.

Leslie

Brief Medical Summary

August 2001—Biopsy of a mass in the right axilla confirmed a tentative diagnosis of inoperable lung cancer. Offered either chemo or radiation palliative therapy. Asked the radiology oncologist whether continuing to play tennis would be therapeutic or possibly aggravating. His answer: "Yes." Gave up tennis.

October 2001—Completed a course of radiation to the right shoulder, providing almost total relief from pain in the right shoulder and arm.

January 2002—Completed a course of radiation to metastatic mass in the right cheek, reducing swelling and discomfort.

March 13, 2002—Without warning, suffered a blackout of unknown duration.

March 20, 2002—Questioned the radiology oncologist about the blackout episode, asking if it was related to current course of radiation treatment or possibly a symptom of disease progression? or totally unrelated? His response: "Yes." Gave up driving.

March 22, 2002—Completed a course of radiation to metastatic muscle mass in left hip, providing relief from pain in hip and rib cage.

March 22, 2002–Consulted with medical oncologist regarding blackout episode; asking if it was related to current course of radiation treatment or possibly a symptom of disease progression? or totally unrelated?" His response: "Yes."

March 28, 2002—Enrolled in hospice program for continuation of drug treatment for pain.

In keeping with his cartoon conclusions, Leslie drew an angelic picture of himself, complete with wings and harp, reposing on a cloud.

"Should'a brought along a few good books and the typewriter !! "

The Passing of a Star

Dear Sylvie,

When Leslie and I returned to the United States in 1985, we met one another's unknown friends and family. Hans, who had been a regular tennis foe, verbal sparring partner, and an admirer and purchaser of Leslie's early artwork, upon meeting me asked, "And what are your talents?"

Without thinking, I replied, "Nothing I can do in public." Stunned silence.

I have my many frustrations and failures and what has seemed to me, especially compared with Leslie, not many talents. But there was a time when I did succeed with a talent, albeit short-lived, for saying and doing the right thing, even in public. From the day I heard the surgeon's "I'm sorry," until the day Leslie passed away, I vowed that whatever he chose to do, I would support him totally. No saying, "Don't you think you should try…" If Leslie asked my opinion, I would offer it, but I would neither undermine nor question his choices, only support him. I lived this vow and did not fail him or myself.

Cancer had visited us before. The first time, I was the hostess. As an unwanted guest, it demands constant attention. It wears you out and makes you long for the life you had before it arrived, and its visit forever changes you. I was diagnosed with cervical cancer, in February 1993. If it's caught early, survival rates start at 80 percent for five years. I was fortunate.

Conducting a staging exam under general anesthesia, the gynecologic oncologist determined that the tumor was deeper than the initial assessment, but found no evidence it had spread to the rectum or bladder. A five-week course of radiation, three-day hospital stay with a radioactive cesium implant, and a concluding hysterectomy were prescribed. As the oncologist was explaining all this to Leslie, he ended the conversation laughing, telling Leslie that, during the staging exam, I had regaled the operating room staff with ribald jokes.

The weekend before the staging exam, I had visited a former neighbor. Bill was an invalid and never failed to brighten my visits with his unique stories and raunchy jokes. During our visit, he told me about Alice, who had gone to her family physician for a checkup. After the exam, the doctor inquired, "Alice, do you smoke after sex?"

Alice thought for a few moments, then replied, "You know, I've never checked."

The other joke was about the Foreign Legion, stationed in the desert for months on end, and their camel, Mabel. Best left unexplained.

I imagine that these were the jokes I shared with the operating staff. I was too embarrassed to inquire.

Except for your mother and aunt and a few close friends, people believed that your grandfather's passing was from the effects of the cancer. It was how he wanted it perceived.

Your mother told me that you know how your grandfather passed away. I want to tell you what occurred that day and why. Please try to remember as you read this, Sylvie, what a dignified man your grandfather was and the courage it took to do what he did.

After my bout with cancer was deemed a victory, Leslie and I read and discussed Derek Humphry's *Final Exit*. We were in agreement that, if either of us had a terminal illness, we, rather than the illness, would choose the timing and method of our exit. Humphry, the founder of the Hemlock Society, promotes dying with dignity.

The Hemlock Society had its own death in 2003, but was resurrected with different leaders and a new name, Compassion and Choices. Their mission is to legalize physician-assisted suicide. In *Final Exit*, Humphry discusses ending one's life through self-deliverance. The recommended method is a drug overdose using pain relievers and sleeping pills, drugs typically prescribed during the latter stages of one's illness to relieve pain and provide comfort. After three months as a Hemlock Society member, one could order explicit books and videos regarding self-deliverance, detailing the suggested dosage and combination of medications to take. A video, entitled *The ABCs of Self-Deliverance,* explains self-deliverance, which medical directives to use, and models discussions with a spouse/partner as to whether there is assistance or just a choice to be with the loved one for support and comfort. It recommends that the patient leave a note and visible signs of a do not resuscitate order.

Leslie wrote in his letter of August 29, 2001, "We all came into this world alone, and that is how we will leave. But, since the fact is that I had little enough to say about how I came in, it is comforting to think I may have something to do about how I exit." He had informed us, through his letters, of what he intended to do from the onset.

It sounds unfeeling to say that we planned for Leslie's death in detail. But we did. Cremation policies had been purchased in 1993. Our names and dates of birth were inscribed on a stone slab, with space allotted for the final dates. If you remember from his farewell service, the slabs stand as sentinels in the cemetery rose garden where his ashes were spread. As we were both well when the cremation plans were made, we had fun with the salesperson. Leslie thought it would be clever to write his obituary using the personal ad format (MWMS, married white male smoker). Over the years, I would jokingly ask him if he had written his obit. Our wills had been executed in 1993, as were our medical directives.

Leslie wrote his obituary on his last birthday. When I read it, I cried and laughed. I still do. Weeks later, I compiled a global e-mail address list of family and friends and created a disk containing the text of his obituary.

Attached is the letter your grandfather wrote to your mother and aunt, informing them of his choice of self-deliverance. He chose not to tell the rest of his family.

Susan

Leslie to Martha and Amy, January 2002

Dear Martha and Amy,

Until the very moment, no one really knows how they would react in a life-or-death situation. We can speculate, logically hypothesize, fantasize in anticipation, but in the actual fact, any prior consideration is lost in the moment. But what about a death or death decision?

A very personal matter.

Modern medicine has provided us with miraculous cures for once-fatal illnesses. Tomorrow will only bring more. Despite the tremendous amount of resources our society devotes to preserving life and finding new ways of doing so, our reasonable choices are limited to today's methodologies.

Lung cancer continues to be one of the more intractable fatal illnesses. Despite its status as a fairly common cause of death and the amount of research devoted to its cure, treatment modalities continue to be painful, ridden with undesirable side effects, and, almost invariably, ineffective. A bleak prognosis for the diagnosed.

As a diagnosee, I do not find the prognosis all bad. Disclaiming a Dr. Pangloss attitude, the timing of the diagnosis, allowing for a bit of time before the final curtain is due, provides me an opportunity to wrap up some final business, put my house in order, and attempt to alleviate some of the burdens that will fall on my successors in life. Not bad for peace of mind.

I have had a reasonably long life—at least, I won't die young. If results were due solely to my efforts, it has proved much more rewarding than I could have imagined or deserved.

I don't fear death. Since I cannot imagine what may exist after life in this world, and such attempts to project fall short of credibility, I refuse to be concerned. Even if my conduct in this life is to form the basis for judgment in a future life, I cannot change my conduct now, and such basis as might exist for said judgment is surely beyond the limitations of our human minds to describe.

Dying, however, is a different matter. We all have had little enough to say in how we began our lives. In some cases, we do have some discretion, active and passive, in how it ends. Though our medical knowledge of life processes and the ability to control them has grown spectacularly in the last fifty years, we have just begun to explore the legal consequences of many of these medical benefits. We cannot legally agree on a definition of life or death! As a litigious society governed by law, delving into these murky legal waters for conflict resolution can be hazardous.

In an effort to avoid any confusion about my intentions and desires, I hope to express myself clearly as to the manner of my dying and ask that, even if you do not agree with them, you recognize them as my own. In light of the above and my knowledge of the experience of those who have suffered death from lung cancer, I have no intention to live up till the bitter natural end.

From what I have known of others' lives, mine has been remarkably free of medical problems. For this, I am most grateful, even if not to what or whom. As a consequence, I have no personal knowledge of chronic pain or physical or mental dependence, and I fear it greatly. In the event the course of this disease leads to such a condition, I would prefer that my life cease and shall willfully take such measure as is available to me to peacefully effect its end.

Mindful of the legal quagmire of liability surrounding assisting death, it is my intention to elect a method that would be reliable, entirely self-administered—without assistance—at a time and place of my own choosing.

Susan is fully aware of my desires and intentions in this matter. She assures me that she will not assist me in effecting them and will not oppose my express desires. Of you, I now ask the same. Should questions arise concerning the circumstances surrounding my death, I would prefer it simply be known as due to the effects of the cancer.

May you console and support each other after the event.

Leslie

Susan to Sylvie, April 20, 2011

Dear Sylvie,

Three years ago, I became a hospice volunteer at a hospital inpatient unit. I have helped bathe many a patient who was dying from lung cancer. Whenever I do, I know that Leslie's decision of self-deliverance was the right choice for him. It would have been anathema for him to "live up till the bitter natural end."

I believe that one should have the right to die with dignity and in the manner one chooses. Physician-assisted suicide should be a legal option; it is not in New Mexico. It is also illegal to assist anyone who chooses self-deliverance. I attended a Hemlock Society meeting in Albuquerque a few months after

Leslie's passing, but the pain and grief were too raw for me to be a contributing member.

Eight years ago, I wrote about what happened the day your grandfather passed away, to help me cope with my grief. Throughout my life, when I have experienced joy or sorrow, writing has enabled me to express my feelings. Unlike your grandfather, who was eloquent in both spoken and written form, I am not eloquent.

May your reading of the attached provide you with an understanding and acceptance of what happened. Please remember his courage and his desire to leave this earth in his own dignified way, just as he had lived his life.

Susan

Susan to Sylvie, April 24, 2011

Leslie told me that he would know when it was time to set a date for his self-deliverance. During January, a tumor appeared on the right side of his face, providing more discomfort and a fixed, crooked grin. Pain medications were increased and another round of radiation alleviated the pain and restored his natural grin. We both knew that time was now marked by weeks rather than months. Although a blackout in March was brief, he deemed it time. The date would be Friday, April 12.

In New Mexico, when a person dies at home, the police, medical examiner, and emergency personnel are called, and an autopsy is required. If a hospice patient dies at home, the hospice nurse can attest to the death and is not required to call other authorities. A siren-less ambulance is sent to the home, and the body is taken to a previously designated mortuary. Leslie was placed on hospice April 1 and assigned a nurse. She came to our home on April 1, delivering liquid morphine for breakthrough pain relief. She explained its use, the initial dosage, and said that the dosage could be increased over time. She returned on April 8 with new prescriptions of morphine in capsule form, as well as Oxycontin and Temazepan, a sleeping pill. The stockpile was complete.

Family leave was granted to me beginning April 1. We spent the last two weeks together, day and night, sharing all we knew of us, never knew, wished we had known—in words, in loving gestures, and even times of humor. Leslie told me that he wanted me to find love again, to remarry. I told him that there would never be anyone else for me and began to cry. He asked, "How can you live without sex?" I quit crying and started laughing. He could do that to me, cause me to cry and then laugh; never the other way, though. He expressed regret that he had not been more demonstrative to me and to his daughters. One evening, watching the shadows of the setting sun creep up the Sandia Crest, he said, "I wish I could take you with me." He held me each night, telling me to let it out. I could not contain my tears. I did not even try.

During the day, he taught me all those things a man would think of that a woman would not: how to turn on and off the controls for the sprinklers, the right mix of fertilizer and bug spray for his roses and his beautiful crepe myrtles, where the tools were, whom to call, whom not to call, and when to tackle things myself. In all seriousness, I remember asking him what last words of wisdom he had for me. He thoughtfully tamped his pipe and replied, "Don't underwater!" He gave away his tennis rackets and arranged for the sale of his treasured Aggie, the 1981 Volkswagen Vanagon in which we had shared so many adventure trips—sightseeing, camping, and the inevitable breakdowns. He wrote last letters to his daughters, several of his dear friends, and one to me, dated April 12, 2002.

Surprisingly, Leslie had not lost many pounds. For months, he had worn warm-up pants, which did not cause pressure around his waist, the area of the adrenal tumor. He loved our New Mexican sun and had a year-round tan, masking what would now be a wan appearance.

It was a warm April, an early spring. Over the past two years, Leslie had pruned a Lady Bank's Rose on the back of our townhome, shaping it into tree form. He had decorated it the past Christmas with twinkling white lights. As we were admiring the tiny yellow blossoms on April 11, he suggested that I have a picture taken in front of it in full bloom and use it as my 2002 Christmas card. I could not bear to do so. He spent a half hour basking in the sun with the garage door open. Everything appeared deceptively normal.

The day before, we visited my mother, for Leslie to share, unbeknown to her, a final good-bye. He cleaned her hummingbird feeder, filled it, and hung it outside in the patio and then sat for twenty minutes. I watched him from the living-room window. The image remains in my memory. When he came back inside, he and Mom had their usual lighthearted banter. He kissed her on the forehead and said, "Good-bye, dear." We rode home in silence. I placed my hand on his knee. Ordinarily, he would have covered my hand with his. This time he did not. I did not intrude on his thoughts on what was his last ride home.

On the evening of April 11, we had a light dinner and, as was his custom, he held the chair for me and then lightly brushed his fingers across my shoulders. It was the same electrifying touch I had experienced every night we were together, except this was the last time. I cannot remember what we said. I do remember that I could barely swallow my food and finally quit trying.

We had each separately watched *The ABCs of Self-Deliverance*. This night, we viewed it together. We were never television watchers, but occasionally we would rent a movie and watch it at home. As Leslie had endured tinnitus for the past decade, we had separate earphones conjoined to one outlet jack, each with our own volume control. I curled up in his lap, being sure I wasn't pressing on his abdomen. I suggested that we create a time frame of when to do what the next morning. This was for me so that I would not break down, but I did not confess that to Leslie. He agreed.

When Leslie and I went to sleep at night, I would curl up with my back to his front, and he would wrap an arm around me. Our last night together, I lay by his side, facing him, until he fell asleep. He told me that he was so glad we had these past months together, that he had the time he did with his daughters and the rest of his family. I stayed awake as long as I could, watching him, remembering, being thankful for us and all we shared.

On April 12, we followed our usual morning routine. I arose first and made the coffee, except this morning Leslie requested tea—less caffeine to dilute the effect of the drugs he would take. I took the hot tea to the garage to Leslie, who was having his pipe and reading the paper. I kissed him good morning, as I always did. When our townhome was built in 1999, Leslie had been able to design an oversized garage. As he never smoked in the house, the garage was his smoking parlor, as well as his drawing studio complete with drafting table and skylight, side door for additional natural light, and a reading chair. The walls were finished, painted, and decorated with a piece of carved wood we brought from Al Baha and a Navajo pictorial weaving that said "Home Sweet Home."

As Leslie shaved and showered, I prepared the breakfast he requested. He wore his favorite winter shirt and his now-familiar warm-up pants. He did not appear to be a dying man. He read the paper as he ate, and I marveled at his composure. Yet, I understood that we both had to complete our normal routine. When he finished eating, he went back to the garage for more of his pipe, and I joined him. He began measuring the liquid morphine into the ceramic cup he used at night to drink his sherry. He stopped and held me, but I broke away because I started to lose control, and I ran upstairs. I slapped myself to get a grip on my emotions. I then went downstairs and followed my schedule and made up the bed in his study.

When I returned to the garage, he was adding the contents of eight sleeping pills to the morphine, as well as four ounces of sherry and two Dramamine, to reduce the possibility of vomiting. He had already swallowed several Oxycontin tablets. It was shortly after 8:00 a.m. when he began drinking this modern-day hemlock. Within minutes, it took effect. I had to help him inside; he could barely walk, and if he could speak, he did not try. Once he was on the bed, he still did not speak, but his eyes were open. I removed his glasses and kissed him, and he shut his eyes.

The last hours, I held him, saying what I could not earlier. I told him how much I loved him, how much he had brought to my life. I said the Lord's Prayer. I told him to let go, go gently into the night, my darling Leslie. I told him I would miss him for the rest of my life; that I would never finish loving him. As his breath became more and more shallow, I prayed that he was not suffering. When he took his last breath, I allowed myself to break down.

In time, I removed his watch, discarded the remaining liquid, and washed the cup. As we had planned, I numbly waited an hour and then called the hospice nurse. When she arrived, I assumed that she would pronounce Leslie dead and the siren-less ambulance would be summoned. When she realized that Leslie had taken an overdose, I didn't know that she would be required to call 911. She did. They called the police, the medical examiner's office, and the paramedics, who arrived with the siren on. At one point, there were eight people present. The police questioned me. The medical examiner questioned me. The remaining drugs were measured and recorded. The hospice nurse called a grief counselor. I wasn't aware that I was in a state of shock. I lied and said I was not present when Leslie took the drugs. They asked me why I removed the cup he drank from, why had I washed it? I told them I was a tidy person, and it had never occurred to me to leave it by the bed. They wanted to know if I would benefit financially from his death. No. They wanted to know if he had left a note. Yes. I produced it and then refused to let them take it, my last letter from Leslie.

Leslie to Susan, April 12, 2002

Dear Susan,

I can no longer contemplate life with what the course of this disease holds in store with any measure of pleasure. I find it preferable that I end it now, while I still feel myself in full control of my own fate.

If it is redundant, it is still worth repeating. I have loved you almost from the day we met. The years of our marriage have been the best of my life. Hopefully, time will mitigate the abruptness of my departure.

Leslie

Hours later, his body was placed in a black bag. I could not bear to watch as they took him away. Sobbing, I went into his closet and buried my head in his favorite jacket. The grief counselor stayed with me after the others left and discussed the hospice grief program. Then, I was alone, as alone as I have ever been.

That night, I put on Leslie's nightshirt, slept on his side of the bed, and, as my pillow, I rolled up the towel he had used in the morning to dry himself. I took half of one of Leslie's remaining sleeping pills.

Electronically, I had sent the obituary Leslie wrote on his birthday to our families and friends, informing them of the passing of a star.

De Mortuis Nil Nisi Bonum

Leslie F. Freeman (1930–2002) died at home on April 12, 2002, of cancer. He predeceases his wife, Susan, who provided him with twenty of the best years of his life, and to whom he leaves his share of their community debts and his private collection (unsold inventory) of artwork; his first wife, Barbara, with whom he raised two daughters; Martha and Amy; three priceless grandchildren, Sylvie, Rosa, and Ethan; two brothers; three sisters; three times six and four times seven nieces and grandnieces, nephews and grandnephews; a host of frustrated senior tennis players still thirsting for revenge; and friends near and far, close and casual, all of whom have helped enrich his life.

A casual student, BA Boston University, MA Whittier College; an irreverent soldier, three-time winner of the PFC rank, separated from the Army Medical Corps under a mutual truce; an indifferent provider over a career of thirty years, primarily engaged in the delivery of health care, who enjoyed his retirement throughout his life while neglecting to earn it; a nonprolific father; inveterate traveler, amateur artist, unpublished author, and rank tennis player. Just a typical life story of a middle-class American boy during an exciting time in US history. He loved it all.

He leaves to posterity a memento disproportionate to his impact on society: his name on a star (fifth magnitude). The Leslie F. Freeman number Aquarius RA 23h 12m 23s D-17' 7" duly recorded in the International Star Registry is clearly visible to anyone with access to the Hubbell Space Telescope.

A Farewell Gathering will be held on Saturday, June 1, 2002, at Sunset Memorial Park at 2:00 p.m., free of charge. Those attending and wishing to assist in spreading his ashes in the Rose Garden are requested to bring a drinking straw and are forewarned: Do Not Inhale! Contributions may be made to Doctors Without Borders, PO Box 94, Toms River, NJ 08754.

Soul Encounters

Susan to Sylvie, April 30, 2011

Dear Sylvie,

Your grandfather suggested that his farewell gathering be held weeks after he passed away. He was being pragmatic and thoughtful, affording everyone time to plan and attend without added expense—cheaper airfare. In keeping with his agnostic beliefs, he didn't want a minister or priest or a church service.

Remember how hot it was on the day of his farewell? I arranged for the use of the mortuary's air-conditioned chapel, thinking he would never know what it cost. I hadn't planned to stand by the door as people entered, it just seemed the right thing to do—honoring Leslie and greeting those who loved and cared for him. Your Aunt Amy thought of placing the long-stemmed red rose, his favorite flower, on a chair, signifying his absence. I wanted to be first to bid him farewell, concerned that I might cry, listening to others' remembrances, and not be able to stop. But I didn't cry, not then.

I had weeks to contemplate what I wanted to say and committed it to paper the morning of his service.

As a young person, grief-stricken over the unexpected loss of a friend, the following comforted me, and it has in facing Leslie's death.

"Love makes people believe in immortality because there seems not to be room enough in life for so great a tenderness, and it is inconceivable that the most masterful of our emotions should have no more than the spare moments of a few brief years."

Leslie was an autonomous person, one who did not need the approval of others. He marched to his own drummer and lived his life in his own way, expressing in written words and intricate drawings what he did not always share in spoken word. He leaves to us those tangible gifts.

Diane, his friend of seventeen years, said in all those years that not once did she hear Leslie say a critical word about another person. His only verbal criticisms of me during our marriage: he did not care for the way I packed a suitcase, and I was born with a fuss gene. There must have been others, but he wisely kept them to himself.

Leslie's gift to me is a greater understanding of life and the ability to love and believe in myself. I was blessed, he was blessed, to have us. We had a wonderful eighteen years together. Thank you, Leslie, for sharing your life with me. I will miss you the rest of mine.

It was your grandfather's request that we gather in the Rose Garden and spread his ashes, as he uniquely described in his obituary. When your grandfather's brother-in-law, an ordained minister, said a prayer—a last-minute request on my part—in the Rose Garden on behalf of the man he had loved as a brother, I heard a distant train whistle and thought it a fitting tribute for Leslie's last trip to places unknown.

Without my knowledge, my brother Pete saved some of the ashes. When we returned home, he spread them around the roses Leslie had planted. It was then that I cried.

Susan

Sylvie to Susan, May 6, 2010

Dear Susan,

As I read your feelings of what happened on the day Grandpa died and now your memories of his service, I can't begin to imagine how hard it must have been for you without him. We flew home, but you, as Grandpa wrote, were left to wash up the dishes and put them away.

Sylvie

Susan to Sylvie, May 11, 2011

Dear Sylvie,

The greatest challenges I have faced during my life are twofold: the loss of those I love and aging; one a challenge of the heart, one of the body. The latter, I can do with grace; the former, I still don't know how to do.

When I was your age, I viewed the world as more black and white than gray. I believed in God but not in life after death. When I pronounced this belief years ago, a friend asked me, "Why believe in God if you don't believe in life after death?" My answer was that I have never been comfortable in this world, so why would I want to keep on living forever and ever. And then I married your grandfather. "Love makes people believe in immortality," the words I quoted at the farewell service, I now began to question rather than discount.

Nothing prepared me for the grief I felt, Sylvie. Leslie and I had planned everything we could to prepare for his death, everything but my grief. I believe that we create our own heaven or hell on earth for it is in our minds. But what do you do once you are in a hell created by grief? How do you get out? For me it was a black pit paved with huge boulders, a place with no markers, no roadmap to navigate a way back to normalcy, assuming one could ever be normal again. I would drive home on a street we had traveled hundreds of times. All I could remember was the last time. The last time I drove Leslie home, the day before his death. Could I ever drive it again without crying? I did not want to eat. I slept only a few hours at a time, waking up to reach for Leslie, my Leslie, who was forever gone. I even missed his snoring. I thought I was going crazy. The day of his death, neither the police officers nor the hospice worker had destroyed the bottle of liquid morphine, the sleeping pills, and the Oxycontin tablets. I had placed them in Leslie's bathroom cabinet, telling myself that, if a year from now I was still in hell, I would take them and end the pain. But I promised myself that I would live out the year.

Before Leslie passed away, I was given the book *Many Lives, Many Masters* by Brian L. Weiss, MD. Dr. Weiss, a psychiatrist, recounts how he had placed a young patient in a hypnotic state to assist her in remembering any childhood traumas. He was startled when she began remembering past lives and even more startled when masters imparted knowledge through his hypnotized patient. The book introduced me to another world of thought: What if we don't die? What if we are immortal?

A few months after Leslie passed away, I attended a church service, seeking, hoping for, some solace. The guest speaker was Dr. Gail Carr Feldman, a psychologist who specialized in grief counseling. Her message was that living through grief can be a creative process. I sensed her empathy and compassion and began consulting with her. She helped me to realize that I wasn't going crazy. She was a person who had not known Leslie and could listen objectively to me. I learned that she believed in life after death, believed that we have lived before and would live again. Toward the end of our sessions, she asked if I would be interested in seeing a medium, a person who channeled messages from souls on the other side. I surprised myself and said yes.

Six months after your grandfather passed away, I went to the home of Joan, a lovely Jewish woman in her mid-sixties. Joan explained that the gift was in her family; her mother had it, as did her daughter. They are able to connect to a higher energy and, through clairaudience, the supposed power to hear things outside the range of normal perception, could channel a message from a soul in the other dimension. Joan told me that it would be a message from the soul I most needed to hear from.

How do I explain the inexplicable? How do I share my changed beliefs, beliefs I would have considered bizarre in my twenties? From the person who didn't believe in life after death to one who now does. I believe that the attached messages are from your grandfather. They span a period of nine years and are loving, instructive, and, at times humorous, just as he was on earth. Fortunately, Joan records the messages, as I cry throughout the channeling.

As Leslie once requested of me, I now ask of you, Sylvie. Suspend your disbelief, and read the attached, with my comments explaining why I believe the messages are from your grandfather.

Susan

Susan to Sylvie, May 15, 2011

Dear Sylvie,

I have italicized the channeled messages, which I transcribed from antiquated cassette tapes. During the first message, Joan's speech slowed, and at times it was difficult to hear. I cannot prove it, no one can prove it, but I know the message was from Leslie.

Channeled Message, October 8, 2002

I, who have left you, always take great care in the measure of your devotion. I, who have watched you grow and have watched you enchant my essence, take great pride in your accomplishments. Do not be afraid to spread your wings in earth years. You are but apart from me in time, apart from each other. There will be no fault-finding. You will subscribe to truth, to energy, to healing, and to love, for truly, love conquers all.

You were not afraid when I needed you to be brave. You did not show fear, even in your younger days. I have myself left. I am connected to you: When you speak I hear you; when you think, I think with you; and when your heart is heavy, I feel you. I feel your grace and your love and your tenderness.

You do not need to seek me out, dear one. I am here, and you are the love. You have my blessing to live, to life.

* * *

Listening to the message was the second-most emotional experience I have had. A belief shattered; Leslie, the soul of my Leslie, exists; he didn't die. How could he communicate with me? What happened to him? Only Leslie would have used the phrase "Take great care in the measure of your devotion." He was wrong, though. I was so afraid his last day, his last day on earth. We are parted physically, but not forever, just for a time? How can I wait? There is now a light in my hell.

Our experiential culture gives little credence to faith. We must see, do, and experience on our own before we believe. How does one believe in an Infinite or Universal Spirit, life after death, or some form of communication with souls, if one cannot prove their existence? We want to believe. Millions watched the television programs of George Anderson and John

Edward's *Crossing Over* and their discernments with souls on the other side. Until the message from Leslie, I had never heard of George Anderson, John Edward, or the Akashic Records. My search began.

The first book I read was *We Don't Die* by Joel Martin and Patricia Romanowski, their story of initially attempting to disprove the physic/medium abilities of George Anderson. They instead became his champions and helped him begin his radio and television shows. Next was *Children's Past Lives* by Carol Bowman, who wrote about her research on reincarnation after her five-year-old son related his life as a soldier in the Civil War. I learned that 66 percent of the world believes in reincarnation. We, in the Western world, are the minority. Western world authorities consider these claims as unproven and studies attempting to prove them as unscientific. Whether we believe it or not, can prove it or not, it is a thought-provoking topic.

I doubt I will be able to persuade you, who are reading this, one way or the other. Thus, I will simply share the recorded messages I have received and comment on why I believe it is Leslie addressing me from the other side.

Twice, I returned to Joan in the next year and a half. These messages were also taped, and, unlike the first, they were long and clearly audible. She told me that no soul had channeled through her as clearly as Leslie. Ordinarily, she is spent by the end of the session; not so with Leslie.

I told a friend, whose husband had passed away within weeks of Leslie, about Joan. She went to Joan, hoping to receive a message from her husband. She told me that her message was vague and brief but not unlike her late husband, as he was a man of few words. His love was shown rather than verbally expressed. She concluded that his message was not out of character, although she was disappointed, as she compared her experience to mine.

Attached is the next message and my explanatory comments. As I believe the messages to be from Leslie, I use his name rather than "soul."

Channeled Message, August 14, 2003

Joan told me that she felt Leslie's presence, he was so strong, wanting to come through before she started channeling. She began, "My *be*loved," paused, and then again, "My belov*ed*."

My eyes were closed throughout; four or five times I heard what sounded like wind chimes. After the channeling, she explained that she has a problem pronouncing beloved and initially placed the emphasis on the *be*. Leslie corrected her, "I said, belov*ed*." The message was so strong and clear this time. She does not remember what is channeled, but she did remember his correction and the sound of chimes.

My beloved, my energy is with you. I feel your sweet presence in the stars. My soul sends manna to your soul—to nourish you and to feed the emptiness that you have felt. Dear beloved, heart of my heart, do not be afraid to go on, for I, who have always loved you, I am still here. Only my corporeal body is gone. I walk with you. I talk to you, and I love you, dear.

I want very much for you to be part of the earth and the earthly life. You have a while before you will come and join me. I have loved you always. I will continue to do so. It is all right for you to love or to like another. I have only blessings and light in my soul for you. In the top drawer of my heart, I write you poems every day. And when you feel the rush of warm wind, it is me, holding you near and caressing you. Do you hear the wind chimes now? They tell of my love for you.

How sweet and how soft the air is here. I am not in pain, dear one. There are many around who support me and love me and love my energy. There are long earth years for you. It is but a day before we will be together again in my time, in my heart's time, and when you cross over, we will no more be parted. But live. Live Susan, live, love, enjoy.

Because my heart ceased beating does not mean that I ceased existing. For I exist. I am. I am in the stars. I am in the sound of the chimes. I am in the laughter, and I am in the garden. And I walk with you, and I hold your hand. Sometimes, I take your elbow, and I guide you, as I guided you in life. There are only three things you need fear: not being able to love, closing yourself off, and holding on too tightly to the past.

It's all right, my own darling; open up to the future. I will be with you. I will not leave you because you choose to go on and live life as it is meant to be lived. This does not in any way separate us. I have loved you in this lifetime. I have loved you in past lifetimes. I cherish you. Let go of the fear. Feel my presence, and abide with me in that which is good and true.

As you choose to go on, it would be very wonderful if you would write what it is you need to write. Whether it is a success on earth or not, it does not matter. The words are to me, and it will reach me, as your presence will reach me. And as you write about us, you will feel me, and our connection will become stronger and stronger. I ask you to be part of what is around that I, my soul, my being-ness, would be very honored if this book were written. Not for money but for love, to let all the world know—and because the earthly vibration from it will help us and bless us and bless the earth.

I am right here. We are circled in light always. If you could but see me as I can see you, you would feel such a sense of peace; it is only a dimension away. And we are but a heartbeat away. Bless you. Don't be afraid.

* * *

Transcribing the recorded message, I remembered the wording in Leslie's pedal hypothermia, cold feet, letter, and compared it with the initial message channeled through Joan. "I, who have *watched you grow* and have watched you enchant my essence." His March 13, 1984, letter read, "I must be crazy to think of marriage again. You've got it made as a bachelor. Self-supporting, even enjoy your own cooking and are a competent housekeeper. Middle-aged women find you attractive; hearts flutter as you pass. Come and go as you please. You have *watched her grow* over the years and marvel to see her blossom, but will she grow on, right past you? Ah, but you have been a part of her as she has grown. Both feeding and *guiding her* and you are already a part of her. See how she stands on her own feet, not too steady yet, but that will come." In the message of August 14, 2003, with Joan, it was channeled, "Sometimes I take your elbow and *I guide you* as I guided you in life."

In an attempt *not to close myself off,* I signed up for a writing class at our favored Ghost Ranch in Northern New Mexico. Leslie and I used to visit the ranch biannually. We camped, hiked, read, and enjoyed the stark, intense beauty of our high, dry desert.

The writing class proved cathartic. One of the assignments was to write about an object using a third-person format. Within a week of Leslie's passing, I had given away his clothing, but I could not bear to part with his shoes. I would periodically dust them—and cry in the process. I thought that, if I wrote about his empty shoes, I might understand why I found it so difficult to part with them.

"Medium, size eight and a half, different colors, shapes, and styles line a wall of her closet. Most are leather, some canvas, a few rubber, even one sheepskin. They are the last items she dons to begin the day; the first she sheds to end it.

"Shoes are foot vehicles marking the timeline of man. Who wore the first ones? Did the Leakeys overlook a fossilized shoe print in the Great Rift Valley? Written chronicles describe the foot garb of the ancients. Jesus's feet were wrapped in palm-frond sandals, his footprints obscured by desert winds. Twelve centuries pass, and the foot armor of the Crusaders following in his steps is now viewed in museums. Bound by dynasty tradition, the slippers of a desirable Chinese woman measure no more than three inches. European aristocrats wore the first pointed toe, high-heeled shoes. A fashion class statement, these shoes weren't meant for walking. Military boots continue to march through the twenty-first century, redefining borders, wearing out hearts.

"We bronze baby's first shoes. We are told not to judge a person until we have walked in their shoes. But if the shoe fits, wear it. Cinderella's did—and she got her prince. Dorothy found her way home.

"There are four pairs of shoes in his closet, nothing else. They are all in a row, dress shoes first, favored sandals last. She cannot bear to part with them. Empty, unmoving, never again to leave a print on her timeline."

In time, I was able to destroy his shoes. I could not give them away, for only he could have filled them.

Thanksgiving passed, Leslie's favorite holiday, and, even though I had been to Joan's a few months before, I needed to hear from him. I wondered, would it be as detailed, as clear as the last message?

Channeled Message, December 8, 2003

Before I got out of the car, Joan was approaching. She told me that Leslie had already told her to tell me, "Happy Christmas." I had brought one of Leslie's drawings to share with Joan.

Blessings. I am so glad you are here. I am so grateful you shared my life. We were so blessed to have each other. I offer you a bouquet of flowers. There are peonies and the most beautiful orchids. But the finest flower is you and your love, which you have given to me.

It's Christmas. Do you remember all the Christmases we shared and all our customs? Do you remember moments when it was icy cold and we were out? There was a china doll I wanted to give you.

You are so special and so loved. Thank you for bringing my painting. All of the vessels are cupped and free of people. It's as if they are waiting to be filled, and the filling of the vessels is the filling of the cup that I hand to you.

Charge on, Susan. Charge on. Don't be afraid to live. I was never afraid because I was with you, and you were never afraid when you were with me. I need to know that you are still not afraid because you know that I am with you.

I travel the realms now. I have seen such wonders. I will share them with you when your time comes, but it is a long way off. It is important for you to sleep peacefully at night so I can come in with you and share with you these many wonders that I have seen. I am allowed to enter the high realms and, dearly beloved, you are at my side. I take your spirit with me. There are some mornings when you wake up tired because I have traveled with you all night. And there are mornings when you wake up rested and peaceful because I have held you in my arms all night.

Change is so hard. As mortals, we do not like change. We encompass security. But I could always handle change.

How I love to nurture you and be there for you. There is a necklace. I bought you a necklace. I want you to wear it. You will get through this Christmas season. A happy holiday, my beloved. I want you to open up. I want you to live. When you are joyful, I feel great joy. And when you are happy, I feel great happiness. I rejoice with you. I will cherish you, and we will share the new year together.

I am on the other side of the glass. I see you. You cannot see me. But I am here, do not doubt it. You can reach out and touch my hand. Trust your senses, trust your feelings. I am with you. My love for you will never cease. All is just a spiritual illusion.

And eat something sweet. Think of me and eat something wonderfully sweet for the new year. My blessings, and think of the sweet life we shared. Feel my presence, dear one. I am here for you.

* * *

I had brought Leslie's drawing of a *dhow* and other boats along the Red Sea shoreline, the empty vessels, to share with Joan. He mentions a necklace. It is an old, thirteen-strand turquoise, *heishi* necklace he purchased from a trader at San Felipe pueblo.

He had a sweet almost every evening. He used to buy boxes of Almond Joys and liked M&Ms with peanuts. He didn't eat much, but oh, he enjoyed his sweets.

I did not show Joan the picture until after Leslie's message. As I previously wrote, I cannot prove to anyone that these messages are from Leslie. I just believe they are. And I will keep trying to explain why I do.

Leslie's pencil drawing of boats along the Red Sea

I began meditating in 2003 primarily to center myself, to increase my spirituality, and to find, if I could, the answer to my purpose in this life. The connection to my beloved soul, the writing, the meditating, and my family, friends, and job served as a ladder out of my hell, the black pit of grief.

The next message is two years after Leslie physically left me. People seem to think that, after a year, grief passes. As I write this, nine years later, there are still times of searing memory twists, the awful ache of missing—however much I believe he exists, that he didn't die. Yes, the intensity diminishes—but the missing, never.

Channeled Message, April 22, 2004

Do you worry that if you begin to live and love again, you will not be with me? Let me put that to rest, dear one. Let me tell you that what we have shared will always remain eternal, and I will wait for you here in this place, by this gate, one more gate. Dearest, we have shared so many gates, so many new pathways. There is yet one more gate, and I will wait for you here, and when you come, we will be together.

My dearest, you must live. I want you to have joy and happiness in this lifetime. Do not settle. It is so easy to settle.

You need to nurture yourself and your ability to love. For if you let that dry out and discern yourself among others as one who has not love to give, you will have destroyed a part of you that I loved so much.

You are very young. I know you feel old at times. But in truth you are very young spiritually and physically. I loved that always about you. I loved to look at your face when I was on the earth plane and touch your face with my hand and outline your face and gently touch each curve on the face plane and the hollow of your neck. That does not go away. I treasure what we had. I treasure our time together.

There are concord grapes growing. Sweet wine is made from those grapes, and our love had sweetness and growth. Beautiful wine was made from the grapes of our love.

You need to accept being happy. Find the happiness within the wellspring that you cherish within yourself and I cherish within you. I am joyful for you. (At this point, Joan's little dog, Rusty, started whimpering in the other room.) *My spirit is here, do not worry about the animal. He feels my spirit.*

I reach my hand to you. You can feel my hand. We were so blessed, and we are still so blessed. Take comfort in this, and release the joy.

Cherish yourself. Cherish what we had. Go on. You do this for me. And it is for this reason it makes me happy.

I want you to travel. I want you to see things through your eyes. And tell me in your dreams what they are like. I want you to laugh and have joy. And in your dreams, you can tell me what this was like. I want you to know that what we had will never die. No matter what you do, it will not die. We will have lifetimes together again.

I bless you, and I love you, dearest. I am with you in peace and in love. And my heart, my heart is with you.

* * *

For the next several years, I did as Leslie suggested, I traveled. I traveled in my work as well as on vacations, taking a train trip across Canada and excursions to Turkey, Morocco, and the Dalmatian Coast. I returned to Shanghai, twenty-two years after my first visit, where cars now outnumber bicycles, trendy garb replaces Chairman Mao outfits, and Westerners are no longer anomalies. But I don't know if I told him all this in my dreams.

After the last reading, I realized that I was becoming dependent on my messages from Leslie, and I purposefully delayed my visits to Joan. After returning in 2007, I planned to visit Joan just once a year.

Channeled Message, March 28, 2007

Before she channeled his message, Joan said that she "felt his presence so strongly, for he has missed you. It's as if sometimes when you speak, something you said resonates with him. His voice comes out in your letters, but his voice comes out when you speak also. His energy is rebounding right now. Something happened that concerned him. He is feeling much better now."

I walk through time and space; my boundaries are limitless. We are connected through the Almighty. We are connected through the limitless prophecy.

I was able to engage in a creative energy switch. There are times when you feel my presence in most unlikely places. There are times when you may go into a store and feel my presence. And yes, Susan, it is my presence, for momentarily, I am that switch. I have been able to accomplish transference of energy. So when you look into the gaze of a sales clerk and you feel me, just for a second, it's me saying hello. I say hello to you more than you ever know. For truly, my love, we never said good-bye. Our love is limitless, like a meadow on a spring day.

I see you now. I am on the other side of the ceiling, and it is glass. But my darling, the glass is one-way, and I see you. I touch you with my mind and with my heart and with my soul. Do not be afraid to acknowledge that. Do not be afraid that I will not cross that bridge and be there for you.

I firmly suspend any disbelief that you may be feeling or doubts that you may have. The valor within you is strong to face another day. I know it is not always easy to face another day and for you to get up and smile and be happy.

I am here. I will not leave you. We will be together. And remember, look for my face. It is out there. Look for me in the young waiter in some small café, maybe holding a cup of your favorite drink. Just for a second, I'm there.

My love to you, dear, my dearest love.

* * *

How do I explain the transference of energy? I cannot, except for a scientific definition. One could say it is my imagination, but after this message, there have been times when I reflect that there was a greeting from Leslie. It is never the exact moment of a stranger's greeting or comment, it strikes me later, sometimes only a few minutes later.

I am grateful that the messages are recorded, as my emotional responses are as intense as the first time. In this message, the words, *"I firmly suspend any disbelief,"* reminded me of Leslie's comments in 1984 from one of his Al Baha letters.

February 4, 1984

Dear Susan,

Once, I think I wrote there are times when it is necessary to suspend belief, to take things on faith, the "Yes, Virginia, there is a Santa Claus" times in one's life. There is also a corollary to this, the times when it is necessary to *suspend disbelief,* the times when fear takes over.

Learn to live in the now, as his next message describes. He begins by addressing me by name, a first.

Channeled Message, October 2, 2008

Susan,

There are choices to be made right now, and there are moments to be treasured. It is very hard to go on when a part of you is gone. I feel as if I took your right arm and your heart. I do not want that for you, dearest. You have a measure of time, you have a measure of space, and of all eternity.

I am learning so much. I want you to feel the peace that I have. I have chosen to give you a gift of healing. I have asked Spirit to hover around you and be there for you. For you were more than my wife, more than my love; you were my beloved. There is a difference between being someone's lover and being their beloved. We felt one another's thoughts. Truly, the two of us were gifted beyond measure.

I wait for you in the mists of time, for you have time yet. You cannot come. It is not your time. I have much learning to do. I have much meaning and much to accomplish on this side.

I want you to feel my presence. I want you to feel joy again. I have given you the gift of joy in this lifetime and in many lifetimes. I have given you the gift of our togetherness, yesterday, and it will be there again tomorrow. But, my beloved, it is for you to know that it remains now. What we shared can never be taken away. Learn to have fun again. Learn to let go of that which is petty; it is beneath you. It is only for you to grasp love and life like a greedy child. For just as a child reaches for the stars, so it is as you reach for my heart, and I embrace you.

In each tree, I am in the leaves; each time you see the birds fly, I am there.

Don't be afraid, Susan. I am with you. I will greet you when you come on the other side. I want you to have a life while you are on the earth plane. It would sadden me if you did not. I want you to let go of the pain, because it is one thing to hold on to the memories that are joyful, but it is quite another to hold on to the pain because it is a reflection of that which you are feeling and which, momentarily, we may have felt together.

Read my words but not obsessively. Let go, and allow yourself to love. Let go, and allow yourself to feel joy again. Money, property— they are only elements of the earth plane.

I am here. You have only to shut your eyes and feel my presence. You have only to have the knowingness and know that I am here. Again, Susan, don't be afraid of love. Cherish each moment and each day. And when you do that, you do it for me, for joy, for my name.

When you pick up a book of sonnets, please remember that I am there. When you read a story, I am in the telling, and when you write the story, you have told our story.

I am here, dearest love. Just love and laugh and enjoy. I want this for you. Remember the magic only exists if you let it. Please remember—this too shall pass. We will be together, and we remain together. So be it, dear, so be it.

* * *

"*Money, property—they are only elements of the earth plane.*" A reminder from the man who once told me we have everything but money. After I made a poor investment in 1996, he penned a message to me on one of his handcrafted cards, "What love has put together, the AMEX, NASDAQ, DJIA, FBI, CIA, and IRS shall neither cement nor put asunder."

From October 2007 until the time of the next channeled message, the stock market had declined 42 percent—with my retirement accounts stepping down in unison. I reemerged from my semiretirement and returned to work. It was an unhappy year; though I enjoyed the work, I struggled emotionally. A year later, I returned to Joan, and his message discusses the difficult time I was having "*here.*"

Channeled Message, September 16, 2009

Hello, Susan,

It has been a long time, too long. But I am not waiting for you, darling. I am just being funny. I want you here. I know you wanted to leave, I feel this. This entity I am channeling through, she did not know this, but you want to leave. You cannot leave; it is not time. I want you to stay in the place where you are. I want you to learn happiness.

Your presence is here to help others. I know that you will be helping someone who will prove to be important to you. There are children around you who need you. I feel that I need to impart this to you. There is some urgency because sometimes I feel the ebb and flow of your soul energy. I feel the throb of your heartbeat sometimes lessen and weaken. Be strong dearest one, be strong for both of us. I have watched you grow. I am with you in every breath you take, in every flower you inhale; with the aroma, I am with you. I tried to help you. I tried to stay with you. There are times you feel as if I am gone. I am not gone permanently. There is work that I have to do on this side. There is much work on the other side that those on your side know nothing about. We do not just sit on a cloud and meditate. We work hard, and my work is very important. So it is when you are in a peaceful space, I can relax and help bring peace to the earth plane.

Susan, don't be afraid. It's all right. It's all right to feel sadness for me, but I want you so to be happy. I want you to rejoice and feel the joy and to feel the bells I send you. When you hear chimes, that is me. When you hear a church bell, I am there. When you walk into the garden, I sit there, and I sit there peacefully. When you put your head down and when you are dejected, I put my arm around you. And we sit as we sat so long ago when first we met. We sit like that; we don't need to talk. There are words that cannot be said, that don't need to be said between two people. There are certain words; for some people those words are restrictive, for other people those words are an opening. For you and me, those words are a beginning. They are part of our beautiful relationship, because words become reality.

What we felt, what we had, is not gone. It is still a reality. Please remember that. I don't want you to feel as if this is over and you will never feel this way again. Because you will.

I wait for you. There is a special place in my heart that reaches out to you. I beg you, dearest one, to stay here, and stick it out. And please, please know that not time, nor space, nor dimensions dim the luster we shared. We are together, Susan; we are blessed.

Each day, pretend that you are happier than you were the day before. And soon it will become a reality. Don't be afraid to speak your truth. Don't be afraid to write about us.

I see you going into old age, and then we will be reunited. But we are reunited now, dearest darling. We are one. So be it, blessed one, so be it. And so it is.

* * *

In reference to my presence helping others, I retired again and resumed my work with hospice. Rarely am I around children, but I had volunteered to join a group, *Tres Islas* Orphanage, in the spring of 2010 to work in various orphanages in Mexico.

Heartbreaking; some of these children were literally left on the orphanage doorstep, others had lived in cardboard hovels. We painted, cleaned, and stocked supply rooms with food and clothing. And from my experience, the personal rewards exceeded the giving.

One could say it is a commonly used statement, but your grandfather often used "so be it." He used it in his October 26, 2001, letter after his explanation of not fearing death, and it is also in the next channeled message.

He humorously states he doesn't just sit on a cloud and meditate. Do you remember his last letter of April 2002? I explained, instead of a pilfered *New Yorker* cartoon, he drew a picture of himself sitting on a cloud.

When I am feeling sad, I do try to remember, and pretend I am happy. It does help, especially when I think I am distracting him from his work.

Channeled Message, November 18, 2010

Before she began channeling, Joan said, "I feel his presence. I felt his presence earlier in the day. I feel the sweetness; he is so glad you came today; he is just so happy you are here. He has been wanting to tell you something. He wants you to know he approves of you and what you are doing with your life."

Dearest darling,

There is only one of you. How wonderful if we could have cloned you and have a world that would know the love that I knew. We were so blessed, and we need to share those moments with each other, with the people around us.

How I long to be able to touch you, to feel your heartbeat, to hear your whisper. How I long for that. And yet it is just as if a moment has passed. And Susan, remember there is no time here. I miss the progression of time. I miss the fact that I could sit down and map out our life together. Our life together was sacred, and it was a treasured moment for you and for me. How blessed we were to have had that. So many people go through many, many lifetimes without ever knowing what we shared. It was truly our blessing. Our life together was a moment in time, in which destiny intervened and brought us together. And that is the truth.

What I have learned here is that we are children. We are children of the light, and if we allow ourselves, we run on the same frequency. We are AC and DC and battery; all of us a part of the light. It is a continuous blanket of light that fills us and fills the earth and brings us together and makes us one.

We shared our flowers; we shared our home; we shared our love. But most of all, dearest darling, we shared each other. The connection we made was the same connection that the heavens make when they come together, when spring enters the earth, when the coldness lifts, and the warmth blankets the earth once more. Mother Nature sure knew what she was doing when she brought us together.

Susan, don't be afraid. Don't be afraid to challenge yourself. I may have to wait for you a long time. But it will be as if it is a day, and I will be here. Do not start a project and be afraid to finish it. You will have many, many projects to finish. You have much of your life left. Much work is undone, much I wanted to complete. When I see you do your work, I know you are completing mine. When I see you lift your face up, I know that you are praying and feeling my presence.

Susan, I am so grateful you are feeling some happiness. My dear one, how I long to tell you how much you have meant to me, how much I cherished the times we spent together, the moments, the life. I am so proud of you.

It is so hard for you to go on without me, I know this. But you are doing me such service. You do such honor to my name. Every day you go on another day and you bring joy to those around you. And you bring love and you bring happiness and you spread that around. Your light is contagious. How well I know that; how well I cherish that. When we were together, I would sometimes look at you and think, I am the luckiest man in the world. I still think that for the time we had and for the moments we shared. Even now. Even when it is dark, the light of your face glimmers above me and around me, and I am enchanted once more.

Don't give up heart. Don't give up hope. Make the book a reality. Go ahead and choose the way you want to do it. Remember: choose your fights, choose wisely what you want to argue about and what is not worth it. There are those who will help you. There are those who will understand.

I have taught you, as you have taught me. Together, we learn anew. Each day, each star in the sky is a reminder of the light and the glow and the love we have shared. Let these moments rest within your heart. Don't be afraid to share them. It is only through sharing that we bring them together. They become alive, as you are alive, as I am alive to you. I, who have loved you so, and being your teacher, I will be with you always. Bless you, dear.

Do you have any questions, Susan? This was the first time he asked a question, and I was startled. It took me a few moments to collect myself. I asked if his work on the other side was proceeding as he wished.

We work very hard. I am pleased. There is much stress in the other world, but I feel as if I am able to accomplish my work. I thank you for your support, your prayers, and your understanding. There are others who work well with me. We are trying to form a radically different, loving world. But I am working hard, thank you. Thank you, Susan, you always supported me. Bless you.

* * *

The last week of his life on earth, Leslie told me he regretted not being more demonstrative to me and your mom and aunt. Yet, he was verbally demonstrative. He did call me dear or darling, and he complimented me almost every day in some manner—how I looked, something I had done. He provided me with a noncritical environment, something a person born with a fuss gene needs.

When I was writing about us, I couldn't wait my self-prescribed year for the next message. Though he loved the Land of Enchantment, he despised the spring winds. It was one of those days when I received this message from Leslie.

Channeled Message, April 26, 2011

Susan, how pleasant! The wind is howling, and yet it is very pleasant here. That's because we are together, as we have been in eternity and through the eternal truth. Beloved, I bless the day I met you. Do you remember? I remember you so well. You seemed so young to my eyes, dear one. You still remain young and vivacious and beautiful. You are my treasure, as I was your life.

I wanted to show you where I am today. I ask this one to open up, to project my vision to you, so you will know where we will be in eternity.

There are marble steps, and the steps are wide. You walk up them, and take my hand. We will walk up the steps together, and you will see and explore my world, as I have had the privilege to see and explore and be part of your world and our world. But dearest one, it is nothing compared with what we will find together. There is a beautiful monarch butterfly ahead of us beckoning. We move off the marble steps and begin to climb down. There is a wide plateau. It is a shade of green that I have never seen on the earth plane, so deep and dark and rich, laced with flowers of every hue and every persuasion, every aroma, every scent. There are daisies, lots of daisies, and violets. There is a magnificent flower, do you like it? It opens up its petals, it is a deep, rich, dark, purple-blue. There are colors here I wish I could describe adequately to you. Come, pull one out, it's all right, it will grow another as you are pulling out that one. I give it to you, take it home, it's with you forever. Whenever you need me, dearest, just look at the flower and remember me and remember this moment.

Over there is music. We have harp music all the time, beautiful, beautiful music and violins and violas. There is a piccolo and a bass. There is a heavenly orchestra.

Come, sit with me, and I will try to tell you how near we are, even though we seem far apart. Susan, we are not far apart. I want you to visualize a looking glass. It's a one-way looking glass. I can see you. I am so close to you I could touch you, but you cannot see me. You have to see me in your mind's eye because your mind's eye is the one-way looking glass for you. For me it is different. I have passed through the valley. I have come out to the other side, and I wait for you. And I will wait for your soul for a long time. I will be here, and we will gather flowers together.

Your book is a testament to our love. The cover should encompass all our beautiful gardens. We shared beautiful gardens together. We shared beautiful moments together, and we shared a beautiful life together.

How inconvenient to be in this predicament, to have had to leave the earth body to be here, because I want to share it with you, and I will share it with you. From this day on, I will keep you with me in the garden. There are trellises, and the trellises have bluebells on them. There are many flowers and rosebuds. There are profusions of roses everywhere you look. There is a flower, a camellia, yes, a camellia, and there are peonies. And the colors, just let your mind go wild because there is no way I can adequately describe the colors to you.

Come sit with me, dearest one. Let us enjoy this garden as we have enjoyed so many gardens and so much love together.

When I met you, I knew you were the right one. It was very difficult for us. It was not an easy situation. How blessed we were that we had each other for as long as we did. You were my gift, and I hope I was yours.

I think you learn not to fear. The only thing I feared was being apart from you. But we are together now. Nothing can separate us, nothing. We are only separate in thought forms. Do you understand that? Only our thought forms are separate. In reality we are together. So you see yourself on the earth plane; you see yourself as a thought form of the earth plane. I see myself as a thought form here, in the outer realms.

Heaven is all around us. What they call heaven is a thought form. There are clouds, and there are mountains, and there is a beautiful, beautiful, beautiful lake. Farther in, there are oceans, and there are places of prayer where people can go and pray. There are no denominations in heaven. There are no Catholics, Protestants, Jews, Indians. We are all one. We are all one, blessed with the thought forms. How sad that they fight over which one is correct: it is immaterial. We are all blessed with the light.

You and I, Susan, dear one, to you whom I love so much, we are one thought form. We are here to teach each other. We are to learn from each other.

I am happy with the work you do. Surround yourself with flowers, surround yourself with music, surround yourself with meditation and teaching. You have much to teach. People will learn from you. Give yourself the credit that you need. Give yourself the credit to do the work you still have to do, to finish your book. No, to finish our book. It is our story. If truth be told, it is stranger than fiction and more beautiful than any story can be.

I will always love you, Susan. I shared this with you; I will bring you back again; I will show you more.

For today, dearest one, please know how much I treasure each moment we spend. And this is a special moment. I feel your pulse and your heartbeat, and we truly are joined and connected. Be blessed, dearest, and know that I am with you. I will never leave you, never. So be it.

* * *

Joan and I talked a bit after this astounding message. She said she remembered the vision; she doesn't always remember the words of his messages. She was surprised that there were no trees in the landscape he presented. She found it odd, no trees. I explained that Leslie felt closed in by trees; it was another reason he felt at home in New Mexico with its vast, open spaces.

I asked her if she had channeled others who were as eloquent and shared as much as Leslie. No. No one had ever channeled as he does. She told me that she usually receives just a few words or images. One she remembered was a statue of what she perceived to be the Virgin Mary. It was painted a bright color. When she described it to the young woman, she began crying and exclaimed, "Yes, it's my mother; she had such a statue in her home."

In this message, Leslie said, *"You were my gift, and I hope I was yours."* Oh, Leslie, what gifts you have given to me! You helped me to believe in myself, to be the winner I didn't realize I am. You taught me not to care so much what other people think, to do what I think is right, even if others disapprove. Age helps. I don't mind if my slacks aren't fashionable or that my favorite coat is fifteen years old. You never used the statement, but you were a proponent of stopping to smell the roses. (I am remembering Lloyd's mother, who told me she stopped to do just that and a snake bit her on the ankle.) I am stopping to smell more roses, Leslie, even if I sometimes think of a snake. On a morning without plans, you used to say, "Let's go for a ride." And off we'd go, exploring our multifaceted Land of Enchantment. You were spontaneous; I was the planner. I am learning to be more spontaneous. By example, you taught me to listen to others, really listen, rather than interject my feelings and memories when another is trying to tell his or her story. And the best of your gifts, you taught me what it is like to be loved completely by another.

Almost all of Leslie's messages tell me not to be afraid. He told me what I need to fear: *not being able to love, closing myself off, and holding on too tightly to the past.* But what does he mean when he tells me not to be afraid? I think the answer is expressed in the following quotation—I wrote it down months ago without acknowledging the source or author's name:

"Fear robs memory of happiness because it dwells upon the limitation and morbidities of the past; it robs the future of pleasurable and enthusiastic anticipation because it casts a shadow of its past into the future; it robs today of the possibility of fulfillment because it denies the good we might experience in the moment in which we live."

And fear cripples the ability to "*live, love, enjoy.*"

Susan

Sylvie to Susan, June 10, 2011

Dear Susan,

I want to believe that the messages are from him, but when I think about it rationally, I begin to doubt. If Joan has been doing these sessions for many years, couldn't she learn to read people, especially if you provide her with information?

I hope I don't hurt your feelings with my doubts, Susan. It's just that I have always thought of people who read tarot cards and hear messages from the dead as a group of charlatans preying on people who are desperate to contact their deceased loved ones.

Sylvie

Susan to Sylvie, June 20, 2011

Dear Sylvie,

How do I know? How do I know it isn't Joan making up these statements, pretending she is channeling messages from a man I love so much, a man she knows I miss so much? She is a lovely woman, Sylvie, but I don't think she is the type to say, "*I wait for you in the mists of time,*" or "*In the top drawer of my heart, I write you poems every day,*" or remember to add "*So be it*" to most of the endings, a phrase I have never used speaking to her. During the channeling, there is never a pause or hesitation for the right word or phrase. In the December 2003 message, he thanks me for bringing his painting. I did bring his drawing into Joan's house; I placed it on her counter, but I didn't show it to her until after the channeling. One could say that none of this is specific, that it is all circumstantial. And yes, this is true. And no, I can't prove it.

Have you ever been in your car, either driving or stopped at a light, and felt that someone was staring at you? And when you look in the direction of the felt stare, you are correct: someone is staring at you. It is that type of feeling. I just know, and I have that staring feeling when Joan is channeling, the feeling of Leslie's presence.

We each gather our own unique cache of experiences, memories, and beliefs to nurture and support us as we travel through our earthly life. And yes, some of the experiences and memories will be painful. Hopefully, what I have shared with you, and all the letters and messages you will one day receive, will add to your cache of beliefs that we don't die.

Sylvie, I have attempted to provide all the reasons why I believe it is Leslie addressing me from the other side, from the outer realm. But I conclude that it is my faith that it is Leslie speaking to me through Joan. When one needs an appropriate saying, especially to describe a heartfelt emotion, Kahlil Gibran is an excellent source: "Faith is an oasis in the heart which can never be reached by the caravan of thinking."

Susan

Sylvie to Susan, June 30, 2011

Dear Susan,

Thank you for your answers. I understand what you mean about the stare. It's happened to me a few times.

Have you shared the messages with Mom? I think she would be interested in reading them, even with her atheist belief.

Sylvie

Susan to Sylvie, July 6, 2011

Dear Sylvie,

I did send the first message to your mom shortly after I received it. I was so overwhelmed and wanted to share with her that he didn't die. She politely dismissed it and admonished me not to become prey to so-called mediums. I did not share any of the other messages with her.

What now seems long ago, I e-mailed you that I had thought about writing our story, our love story, and what happens when we pass away. I have more than thought about it; I have written it two times, and I am working on the third. I started a year after he passed away; the first telling only contained a few of his messages. As your mom hasn't shared any of your grandfather's letters with you, you might not know that she edited a book of his essays in 1998 entitled *Ad Finitum*. The first copy, he inscribed, "To Susan, first and always." Only a small portion of his letters are included in what I have written and sent to you, Sylvie. He channeled in his last message, *"Give yourself the credit to do the work you still have to do, to finish your book. No, to finish* our *book. It is our story."*

It is a tribute to him that I have written our story. I had to write it and share what I learned, am learning, from loving him. When I thanked Leslie for his gifts to me, they were of the earth plane. His gifts have expanded to give me a glimpse of what it is like on the other side: he can transfer his energy in order to speak to me; he can explain there are no denominations in heaven; and he can teach me about thought forms.

Susan

Sylvie to Susan, July 15, 2011

Dear Susan,

Even though I have doubts about the messages, I do believe that your story *"is stranger than fiction and more beautiful than any story can be."* Thank you for sharing it with me and for someday leaving me the letters. Have you given your manuscript a title?

Sylvie

Susan to Sylvie, July 25, 2011

Dear Sylvie,

I have entitled it *I, Who Have Left You,* the words of his first message, the words that let me know he never left me.

Susan

Acknowledgments

First and foremost, my thanks to my beloved Leslie, who guided me on earth as he continues to do from the outer realm. To my friends who offered their constant support and encouragement: Jane Champagne, Ida Kelly, Lorrie Griego, Lori Galves, Judy Katz, Michelle Wiley, Susan Williams, and my sister, Christine Gibson. Thank you, Joan, for your gift. And lastly to RJ, I give you my thanks for your understanding, if not belief, during this journey.

About the Author

Susan Freeman was a rather incompetent farmhand before she married Leslie Freeman. For their honeymoon, they spent a year and a half working in a remote hospital in the mountains of Saudi Arabia. She is a retired CPA and a dedicated hospice volunteer. She lives in Albuquerque, New Mexico.